101 Life-Skills Discussion Topics

David Cowan
Susanna Palomares

Cover design: Dave Cowan

ISBN-10: 1-56499-090-7

ISBN-13: 978-1-56499-090-7

INNERCHOICE Publishing
15079 Oak Chase Court
Wellington, FL 33414

www.InnerchoicePublishing.com

Contents

Learning and Creativity **83**

Introduction

In order for students to be ready for a fulfilling, productive adult life, they need to learn how to get along in the world. They need to know who they are, how they function, and how they relate to others. They also need to believe in themselves.

Human beings are whole people—not a collection of parts. Feelings, thoughts, and behaviors are interactive, relating to one another in a multitude of ways. All have to be included when young people strive for self-understanding, growth, and the development of life-skills. Throughout this book, a wide variety of topics representing a broad range of experiences is offered in order to approach the goal of life-skill development.

This book combines carefully selected discussion **topics** along with guidelines for establishing a discussion **process** that creates the needed emotional safety for students to fully engage in discussion with other students and their teacher or counselor. This combination of discussion topics and specific procedures to follow is called the Sharing Circle.

Simply described, the Sharing Circle is a small-group discussion in which participants listen carefully to one another as they take turns verbally responding to a specific topic, and then freely discuss any individual and collective insights that are gained from sharing.

The Sharing Circle always follows the same process even though the topic for discussion changes. In its broadest sense, the circle session is designed to facilitate communications between participants. Circle sessions are designed to help students acquire a broad range of life skills by allowing them the opportunity to explore aspects of human life, appreciate themselves and others as developing persons, practice effective communication skills, and develop empathy for others.

No matter what is going on in counseling groups or the classroom, regardless of the curricular content, the circle session helps students make relevant connections to their own lives, while facilitating positive interaction, personal insight, self-awareness, and mastery. By promoting personal competence in each student relative to the topic of the discussion, the circle session promotes the skills and competencies that build and strengthen life-skills.

It is possible to effect a positive change in the emotional and social development of people when they are young by intervening in their lives in such a way as to ensure awareness, social facility, and self-esteem. This kind of intervention is the purpose of these discussion topics, which relates to three critical areas of human functioning: (1) awareness (of the feelings, thoughts, and behavior of self and others); (2) social relations (how individuals get along with other people); and (3) self-esteem (how individuals perceive their worth and worthiness). For purposes of brevity these areas are called **Awareness**, **Social Interaction**, and **Mastery**. They comprise the underlying theoretical components of the Sharing Circles. These discussion topics are built on a developmental progression from Awareness through Social Interaction to Mastery.

Students relate to others verbally in the circle sessions as each topic is discussed. They also learn to listen. Sharing Circles provide practice in basic communication skills, while subject matter relating to relevant life issues is being discussed. This provides positive experiences which offer students the opportunity to grow in awareness, to learn more about effective modes of social interaction, and to feel more masterful (self-confident).

Regular participation in meaningful discussion serves as a way of developing, maintaining, and enhancing life skills. The experiences gained from participating in these Sharing Circle discussion topics can contribute to the reservoir of strength from which we may draw when difficult life circumstances occur.

The following are descriptions of the three growth areas of the program.

Awareness

Awareness is a critical element in life-skill development. Aware people do not hide things from themselves. They are in touch with the inner world of their feelings and thoughts, and they are in control of their actions—and they understand that other people feel, think, and behave too. They are also in touch with the reality of the past, the possibilities of the future, and the certainty of the present. Awareness allows individuals to order their lives flexibly and effectively on a moment-to-moment basis.

By contrast, unawareness of what is going on in one's inner and/or outer worlds sets the stage for lack of congruence between what one believes or feels and how one behaves. Feelings of isolation ("I'm the only one who's ever felt like this before.") occur when people are unaware that everyone experiences the same triad of human functioning (feeling, thinking, and behaving) that they do. Unaware people are not in charge of their own lives. By default, their courses are plotted by others or by parts of themselves they have not recognized.

We hope to demonstrate experientially to students, through regular discussions, that everyone experiences all the emotions. These circle session topics provide opportunities for students to experience and discuss their emotions in an accepting and nonthreatening atmosphere. Students discover that emotions cannot be judged right or wrong, good or bad, in a moral sense. They simply are. To try to negate one's feelings or attempt to take away a feeling in someone else only compounds the situation—as neuroses, insomnia, and miscommunication between persons testifies. For this reason the feelings of each student are focused on and accepted in every session.

Similar to a feeling, a thought, in and of itself, can hurt no one. The discussion phase of each session enables students to share their thoughts in a constructive manner. They become aware that even divergent thoughts may be discussed without fear. Students realize that their ability to think is a great power, and may be used constructively or destructively in a multitude of ways. Through their participation, students become more aware of how often they personally use their thought processes to make life meaningful and productive.

Social Interaction

People effective in their social interactions are capable of understanding other people. They know how to interact with others flexibly, skillfully, and responsibly, without sacrificing their own needs and integrity. They have a good sense of timing and are effective at being heard and making needed changes in their environment. These people can process nonverbal as well as verbal messages of others, and they realize that people have the power to affect one another. They are aware, not only of how others affect them, but also of the effect of their behavior on others, and they take accompanying responsibility for their actions.

Without skills in social interaction, individuals confuse situations and give inappropriate responses. They lack positive communication skills and are unaware of how their actions affect others.

Students deal with other people every day—their peers and significant adults. They need positive interpersonal experiences and information in the social realm in order to build healthy relationships. If they are fortunate, students are surrounded by people who give them positive attention. In the case of people older than they, it is highly desirable that healthy, responsible behavior be modeled. If students are listened to, if their feelings are accepted, and if they learn how to do this with others, they are then able to develop positive, caring, and trusting relationships.

By their format and process, Sharing Circles allow students to practice positive modes of communication and transfer them to other situations.

By participating in Sharing Circles, students are given the opportunity to discuss what goes into a relationship that makes it friendly, caring, and trusting. Further, students explore problem areas in varied human settings. Society has an ideal view of how people should ultimately behave, but no formal structure that defines or describes the intermediate steps. Sharing Circles develop and nurture an understanding of those intermediate steps.

Mastery

Self-confident people believe in themselves; they perceive themselves as being "OK." They are not debilitated by knowledge of their weaknesses, but have a healthy degree of self-esteem and a feeling of mastery or self-confidence. They try new challenges and do not strongly fear failure. It is likely that they have experienced success more than failure, and probably when they were successful, a significant person noted it and commented on it to them.

Individuals are likely to achieve mastery in their endeavors when they have a feeling of mastery about themselves. Generally, people who believe in themselves are the ones who continue to succeed, and the more they succeed, the more they believe in themselves. Thus, a beneficial cycle is created.

The ways in which significant others respond to what we do plays a critical role in whether or not we see ourselves as masterful. If others let us know they recognize our efforts and comment positively when we try or succeed, our awareness that we do have capabilities increases. Conversely, without favorable comment we are less aware of our capabilities, even if we experience success. This explains why so many brilliant people do not regard themselves as such. Rather, they are painfully aware of their limitations and shortcomings and miss many opportunities to actualize their potential. Our culture has numerous ways of causing us to focus on our weaknesses rather than our assets and abilities.

Through participating in Sharing Circles, students are routinely encouraged to explore their own successes and hear positive comments about their efforts. All the topics are designed to heighten students' awareness of their own and others' successes. Failure is a reality that is also examined. The objective, however, is not to remind students that they have failed; instead these activities enable them to see that falling short is a common, universal experience.

History speaks to us of many effective and capable individuals who found great success in their endeavors. Some, however, achieved success for themselves at the expense of others. They exercised their abilities and powers irresponsibly. By focusing on their positive behaviors and accomplishments, students recognize the rewards that can be gained when one behaves responsibly. Cooperation vs. competition is another issue addressed by the mastery portion of the program. As equitably as possible, the program's structure attempts to meet the needs of all students in the group. Everyone's feelings are accepted.

Comparisons and judgments are not made. The circle is not another competitive arena, but is guided by a spirit of cooperation. When students practice fair, respectful, noncompetitive interaction with each other, they benefit from the experience and are likely to employ these responsible behaviors in other life situations.

The Sharing Circle topics presented in this book have been developed to help students deal with such matters as improving their learning habits, taking pride in their accomplishments, dealing rationally with disappointments and problems, and making workable decisions. We hope to help students become responsibly competent with a repertoire of effective life-skills.

How to Set Up Sharing Circle Discussions

Group Size and Composition

Sharing Circles are a time for focusing on students' contributions in an unhurried fashion. For this reason, each Sharing Circle group needs to be kept relatively small—eight to twelve usually works best. Once they move beyond the primary grades, students are capable of extensive verbalization. You will want to encourage this, and not stifle them because of time constraints.

Each group should be as **heterogeneous** as possible with respect to sex, ability, and racial/ethnic background. Sometimes there will be a group in which all the students are particularly reticent to speak. At these times, bring in an expressive student or two who will get things going. Sometimes it is necessary for practical reasons to change the membership of a group. Once established, however, it is advisable to keep a group as stable as possible.

Length and Location of Sharing Circles

Depending on the number, the ages and the verbal expressiveness of the students in a Sharing Circle, some circle sessions can last 20 to 30 minutes. At first, students tend to be reluctant to express themselves fully because they do not yet know that the circle is a safe place. Consequently your first sessions may not last more than 10 to 15 minutes. Generally speaking, students become comfortable and motivated to speak with continued experience.

In secondary classrooms circle sessions may be conducted at any time during the class period. Starting circle sessions at the beginning of the period allows additional time in case students become deeply involved in the topic. If you start circles late in the period, make sure the students are aware of their responsibility to be concise.

In elementary classes, any time of day is appropriate for Sharing Circles. Some teachers like to set the tone for the day by beginning with circles; others feel it's a perfect way to complete the day and to send the children away with positive feelings.

Sharing Circles may be carried out wherever there is room for students to sit in a circle and experience few or no distractions. Some leaders prefer to have students sit in chairs, others on the floor. Some leaders conduct sessions outdoors, with students seated in a secluded, grassy area.

How to Get Started

Teachers and counselors have used numerous methods to involve students in the circle process. What works well for one leader or class does not always work for another. Here are two basic strategies leaders have successfully used to set up Sharing Circle groups. Whichever you use, we recommend that you post a chart listing the Sharing Circle rules and procedures to which every participant may refer.

1. Start one group at a time, and cycle through all groups. If possible, provide an opportunity for every student to experience a Sharing Circle in a setting where there are no disturbances. This may mean arranging for another staff member or aide to take charge of the students not participating in the circle. Non-participants may work on course work or silent reading, or, if you have a cooperative librarian, they may be sent to the library to work independently or in small groups on a class assignment. Repeat this procedure until all of the students have been involved in at least one circle session.

Next, initiate a class discussion about the circle sessions. Explain that from now on you will be meeting with each Sharing Circle group in the classroom, with the remainder of the class present. Ask the students to help you plan established procedures for the remainder of the class to follow.

Meet with each Sharing Circle group on a different day, systematically cycling through the groups. In grades 3 and up, you may wish to start student leadership training after you've completed a number of circles. In each group, allow a student the opportunity to lead the session as you sit beside him or her, acting as leader-trainer. In time, student-led groups may meet independently at staggered times during the period, or they may meet simultaneously in different parts of the room while you circulate. Eventually you should be able to be a participant in the student-led groups. For more information on student leadership, refer to the next chapter, "Training Student Leaders."

2. Combine inner and outer circles.
Meet with one Sharing Circle group while another group listens and observes as an outer circle. Then have the two groups change places, with the students on the outside becoming the inner circle, and responding verbally to the topic. If you run out of time in secondary classrooms, use two class periods for this. Later, a third group may be added to this alternating cycle. The end product of this arrangement is two or more groups (comprising everyone in the class) meeting together simultaneously. While one group is involved in discussion, the other groups listen and observe as members of an outer circle. *Invite the members of the outer circle to participate in the review and discussion phases of the circle.*

What To Do With the Rest of the Class

If you are working with a classroom or large group of students, a number of arrangements can be made for students who are not participating in Sharing Circles. Here are some ideas:

- Arrange the room to ensure privacy. This may involve placing a circle of chairs or carpeting in a corner, away from other work areas. You might construct dividers from existing furniture, such as bookshelves or screens, or simply arrange chairs and tables in such a way that the circle area is protected from distractions.

- Involve aides, counselors, parents, or fellow teachers. Have an aide conduct a lesson with the rest of the class while you meet with a circle group. If you do not have an aide assigned to you, use auxiliary staff or parent volunteers.

- Have students work quietly on subject-area assignments in pairs or small, task-oriented groups.

- Utilize student aides or leaders. If the seat-work activity is in a content area, appoint students who show ability in that area as "consultants," and have them assist other students.

- Give the students plenty to do. List academic activities on the board. Make materials for quiet individual activities available so that students cannot run out of things to do and be tempted to consult you or disturb others.

- Make the activity of students outside the Sharing Circle enjoyable. When you can involve the rest of the class in something meaningful to them, students will probably be less likely to interrupt the circle.

- Have the students work on an ongoing project. When they have a task in progress, students can simply resume where they left off, with little or no introduction from you. In these cases, appointing a "person in charge," "group leader," or "consultant" is wise.

- Allow individual journal-writing. While a Sharing Circle is in progress, have the other students make entries in a private (or share-with-teacher-only) journal. The topic for journal writing could be the same topic that is being discussed in the Sharing Circle. Do not correct the journals, but if you read them, be sure to respond to the entries with your own written thoughts, where appropriate.

How to Lead a Sharing Circle Discussion

This section is a thorough guide for conducting Sharing Circles. It covers major points to keep in mind and answers questions which will arise as you begin using the program. Please remember that these guidelines are presented to assist you, not to restrict you. Follow them, and trust your own leadership style at the same time.

The Sharing Circle is a structured communication process that provides students a safe place for learning about life and developing important aspects of social-emotional learning.

First, we'll provide a brief overview of the process of leading a Sharing Circle and then we'll cover each step in more detail.

A Sharing Circle begins when a group of students and the adult leader sit down together in a circle so that each person is able to see the others easily. The leader of the Sharing Circle briefly greets and welcomes each individual, conveying a feeling of enthusiasm blended with seriousness.

When everyone appears comfortable, the leader takes a few moments to review the Sharing Circle Rules. These rules inform the students of the positive behaviors required of them and guarantees the emotional safety and security, and equality of each member.

After the students understand and agree to follow the rules, the leader announces the topic for the session. A brief elaboration of the topic follows in which the leader provides examples and possibly mentions the topics relationship to prior topics or

to other things the students are involved in. Then the leader re-states the topic and allows a little silence during which circle members may review and ponder their own related memories and mentally prepare their verbal response to the topic. (The topics and elaborations are provided in this curriculum.)

Next, the leader invites the circle participants to voluntarily share their responses to the topic, one at a time. No one is forced to share, but everyone is given an opportunity to share while all the other circle members listen attentively. The circle participants tell the group about themselves, their personal experiences, thoughts, feelings, hopes and dreams as they relate to the topic. Most of the circle time is devoted to this sharing phase because of its central importance.

During this time, the leader assumes a dual role—that of leader and participant. The leader makes sure that everyone who wishes to speak is given the opportunity while simultaneously enforcing the rules as necessary. The leader also takes a turn to speak if he or she wishes.

After everyone who wants to share has done so, the leader introduces the next phase of the Sharing Circle by asking several discussion questions. This phase represents a transition to the intellectual mode and allows participants to reflect on and express learnings gained from the sharing phase and encourages participants to combine cognitive abilities and emotional experiencing. It's in this phase that participants are able to crystallize learnings and to understand the relevance of the discussion to their daily lives. (Discussion questions for each topic are provided in this curriculum.)

When the students have finished discussing their responses to the questions and the session has reached a natural closure, the leader ends the session. The leader thanks the students for being part of the Sharing Circle and states that it is over.

What follows is a more detailed look at the process of leading a Sharing Circle.

Steps for Leading a Sharing Circle

1. **Welcome Sharing Circle members**
2. **Review the Sharing Circle rules ***
3. **Introduce the topic**
4. **Sharing by circle members**
5. **Ask discussion questions**
6. **Close the circle**

*optional after the first few sessions

1. Welcome Sharing Circle members

As you sit down with the students in a Sharing Circle group, remember that you are not teaching a lesson. You are facilitating a group of people. Establish a positive atmosphere. In a relaxed manner, address each student by name, using eye contact and conveying warmth. An attitude of seriousness blended with enthusiasm will let the students know that this Sharing Circle group is an important learning experience—an activity that can be interesting and meaningful.

2. Review the Sharing Circle rules

At the beginning of the first Sharing Circle, and at appropriate intervals thereafter, go over the rules for the circle. They are:

Sharing Circle Rules

- Everyone gets a turn to share, including the leader.
- You can skip your turn if you wish.
- Listen to the person who is sharing.
- There are no interruptions, probing, put-downs, or gossip.
- Share the time equally.

From this point on, demonstrate to the students that you expect them to remember and abide by the ground rules. Convey that you think well of them and know they are fully capable of responsible behavior. Let them know that by coming to the Sharing Circle they are making a commitment to listen and show acceptance and respect for the other students and you. It is helpful to write the rules on chart paper and keep them on display for the benefit of each Sharing Circle session.

3. Introduce the topic

State the topic, and then in your own words, elaborate and provide examples as each lesson in this book suggests. The introduction or elaboration of the topic is designed to get students focused and thinking about how they will respond to the topic. By providing more than just the mere statement of the topic, the elaboration gives students a few moments to expand their thinking and to make a personal connection to the topic at hand. Add clarifying statements of your own that will help the students understand the topic. Answer questions about the topic, and emphasize that there are no "right" responses. Finally, restate the topic, opening the session to responses (theirs and yours). Sometimes taking your turn first helps the students understand the aim of the topic. The introductions, as written in this book, are provided to give you some general ideas for opening the Sharing Circle. It's important that you adjust and modify the introduction and elaboration to suit the ages, abilities, levels, cultural/ethnic backgrounds and interests of your students.

4. Sharing by circle members

The most important point to remember is this: The purpose of these Sharing Circles is to give students an opportunity to express themselves and be accepted for the experiences, thoughts, and feelings they share. Avoid taking the action away from the students. They are the stars!

5. Ask discussion questions

Responding to discussion questions is the cognitive portion of the process. During this phase, the leader asks thought-provoking questions to stimulate free discussion and higher-level thinking. Each Sharing Circle lesson in this book concludes with several discussion questions. At times, you may want to formulate questions that are more appropriate to the level of understanding in your students—or to what was actually shared in the circle. If you wish to make connections between the topic and your content area, ask questions that will accomplish that objective and allow the answering of the discussion questions to extend longer. We have left a space on each page for you to note significant other questions that you create and find effective.

6. Close the circle

The ideal time to end a Sharing Circle is when the discussion question phase reaches natural closure. Sincerely thank everyone for being part of the circle. Don't thank specific students for speaking, as doing so might convey the impression that speaking is more appreciated than mere listening. Then close the group by saying, "This Sharing Circle is over," or "OK, that ends our circle."

Reviewing what is shared (An optional step)

Besides modeling effective listening (the very best way to teach it) and positively reinforcing students for attentive listening, a review can be used to deliberately improve listening skills in circle members. If you choose to conduct a review, introduce it after the sharing phase and before you ask the discussion questions.

Reviewing is a time for reflective listening, when circle members feed back what they heard each other say during the sharing phase of the circle. Besides encouraging effective listening, reviewing provides Sharing Circle members with additional recognition. It validates their experience and conveys the idea, "you are important," a message we can all profit from hearing often.

To review, a circle member simply addresses someone who shared, and briefly paraphrases what the person said ("John, I heard you say...."). Be sure that everyone who shared gets a review.

The first few times you conduct reviews, stress the importance of checking with the speaker to see if the review accurately summarized the main things that were shared. If the speaker says, "No," allow him or her to make corrections. Stress too, the importance of speaking directly to the speaker, using the person's name and the pronoun "you," not "he" or "she." If someone says, "She said that...," intervene as promptly and respectfully as possible and say to the reviewer, "Talk to Betty... Say you." This is very important. The person whose turn is being reviewed will have a totally different feeling when talked to, instead of about.

Note: Remember that the review is optional and is most effective when used occasionally, not as a part of every circle.

More about Sharing Circle Steps and Rules

The next few paragraphs offer further clarification concerning leadership of Sharing Circles.

Who gets to talk? Everyone. The importance of acceptance cannot be overly stressed. In one way or another practically every ground rule says one thing: accept one another. When you model acceptance of students, they will learn how to be accepting. Each individual in the group is important and deserves a turn to speak if he or she wishes to take it. Equal opportunity to become involved should be given to everyone in the Sharing Circle.

Members should be reinforced equally for their contributions. There are many reasons why a leader may become more enthused over what one student shares than another. The response may be more on target, reflect more depth, be more entertaining, be philosophically more in keeping with one's own point of view, and so on. However, students need to be given equal recognition for their contributions, even if the contribution is to listen silently throughout the session.

In most of the Sharing Circles, plan to take a turn and address the topic, too. Students usually appreciate it very much and learn a great deal when their teachers, counselors, and other adults are willing to tell about their own experiences, thoughts, and feelings. In this way you let your students know that you acknowledge your own humanness.

Does everyone have to take a turn? No. Students may choose to skip their turns. If the circle becomes a pressure situation in which the members are coerced in any way to speak, it will become an unsafe place where participants are not comfortable. Meaningful discussion is unlikely in such an atmosphere. By allowing students to make this choice, you are showing them that you accept their right to remain silent if that is what they choose to do.

As you begin the circle, it's important to remember that it's not a problem if one or more students decline to speak. If you are imperturbable and accepting when this happens, you let them know you are offering them an opportunity to experience something you think is valuable, or at least worth a try, and not attempting to force-feed them. You as a leader should not feel compelled to share a personal experience in every session, either. However, if you decline to speak in most of the sessions, this may have an inhibiting effect on the students' willingness to share.

A word should also be said about how this ground rule has sometimes been carried to extremes. Sometimes leaders have bent over backwards to let students know they don't have to take a turn. This seeming lack of enthusiasm on the part of the leader has caused reticence in the students. In order to avoid this outcome, don't project any personal insecurity as you lead the session. Be confident in your proven ability to work with students. Expect something to happen and it will.

Some leaders ask the participants to raise their hands when they wish to speak, while others simply allow free verbal sharing without soliciting the leader's permission

first. Choose the procedure that works best for you, but do not call on anyone unless you can see signs of readiness. And do not merely go around the circle.

Some leaders have reported that their first group fell flat—that no one, or just one or two students, had anything to say. But they continued to have groups, and at a certain point everything changed. Thereafter, the students had a great deal to say that these leaders considered worth waiting for. It appears that in these cases the leaders' acceptance of the right to skip turns was a key factor. In time most students will contribute verbally when they have something they want to say, and when they are assured there is no pressure to do so.

Sometimes a silence occurs during a session. Don't feel you have to jump in every time someone stops talking. During silences students have an opportunity to think about what they would like to share or to contemplate an important idea they've heard. A general rule of thumb is to allow silence to the point that you observe group discomfort. At that point move on. Do not switch to another topic. To do so implies you will not be satisfied until the students speak. If you change to another topic, you are telling them you didn't really mean it when you said they didn't have to take a turn if they didn't want to.

If you are bothered about students who attend a number of sessions and still do not share verbally, reevaluate what you consider to be involvement. Participation does not necessarily mean talking. Students who do not speak are listening and learning.

How can I encourage effective listening?
The Sharing Circle is a time (and place) for students and leaders to strengthen the habit of listening by doing it over and over again. No one was born knowing how to listen effectively to others. It is a skill like any other that gets better as it is practiced. In the immediacy of the Sharing Circle the members become keenly aware of the necessity to listen, and most students respond by expecting it of one another.

In these Sharing Circles, listening is defined as the respectful focusing of attention on individual speakers. It includes eye contact with the speaker and open body posture. It eschews interruptions of any kind. When you lead a circle, listen and encourage listening in the students by (1) focusing your attention on the person who is speaking, (2) being receptive to what the speaker is saying (not mentally planning your next remark), and (3) recognizing the speaker when she finishes speaking, either verbally ("Thanks, Shirley") or nonverbally (a nod and a smile).

To encourage effective listening in the students, reinforce them by letting them know you have noticed they were listening to each other and you appreciate it.

How can I ensure the students get equal time? When group members share the time equally, they demonstrate their acceptance of the notion that everyone's contribution is of equal importance. It is not uncommon to have at least one dominator in a group. This person is usually totally unaware that by continuing to talk he or she is taking time from others who are less assertive. An important social skill is knowing how you affect others in a group and when dominating a group is inappropriate behavior.

Be very clear with the students about the purpose of this ground rule. Tell them at the outset how much time there is. When it is your turn, always limit your own contribution. If someone goes on and on, do intervene (dominators need to know what they are doing), but do so as gently and respectfully as you can.

What are some examples of put-downs?
Put-downs convey the message, "You are not okay as you are." Some put-downs are deliberate, but many are made unknowingly. Both kinds are undesirable in a Sharing Circle because they destroy the atmosphere of acceptance and disrupt the flow of sharing and discussion. Typical put-downs include:

- over questioning.
- statements that have the effect of teaching or preaching
- advice giving
- one-upsmanship
- criticism, disapproval, or objections
- sarcasm
- statements or questions of disbelief

How can I deal with put-downs? There are two major ways for dealing with put-downs: preventing them from occurring and intervening when they do.

Going over the rules with the students at the beginning of each Sharing Circle, particularly in the earliest sessions, is a helpful preventive technique. Another is to reinforce the students when they adhere to the rule. Be sure to use non patronizing, non evaluative language.

Unacceptable behavior should be stopped the moment it is recognized by the leader. When you become aware that a put-down is occurring, do whatever you ordinarily do to stop destructive behavior. If one student gives another an unasked-for bit of advice, say for example, "Jane, please give Alicia a chance to tell her story." To a student who interrupts say, "Ed, it's Sally's turn." In most cases the fewer words, the better—students automatically tune out messages delivered as lectures.

Sometimes students disrupt the group by starting a private conversation with the person next to them. Touch the offender on the arm or shoulder while continuing to give eye contact to the student who is speaking. If you can't reach the offender, simply remind him or her of the rule about listening.

If students persist in putting others down or disrupt the circle, ask to see them at another time and hold a brief one-to-one conference, urging them to follow the rules. Suggest that they reconsider their membership in the group. Make it clear that if they don't intend to honor the rules, they are not to come to the group.

How can I keep students from gossiping? Periodically remind students that using names and sharing embarrassing information in a Sharing Circle is not acceptable. Urge the students to relate personally to one another, but not to tell intimate details of their lives.

What should the leader do during the discussion question phase? Conduct this part of the process as an open forum, giving students the opportunity to discuss a variety of ideas and accept those that make sense to them. Don't impose your opinions

on the students, or allow the students to impose theirs on one another. Ask open-ended questions, encourage higher-level thinking, contribute your own ideas when appropriate, and act as a facilitator.

In Conclusion: The Two Most Important Things to Remember

No matter what happens in a Sharing Circle session, the following two elements are the most critical:

1. Everyone gets a turn.

2. Everyone who takes a turn gets listened to with respect.

What does it mean to get a turn? Imagine a pie divided into as many pieces as there are people in the group. Telling the students that everyone gets a turn, whether they want to take it or not, is like telling them that each one gets a piece of the pie. Some students may not want their piece right away, but they know it's there to take when they do want it. As the teacher or counselor, you must protect this shared ownership. Getting a turn not only represents a chance to talk, it is an assurance that every member of the group has a "space" that no one else will violate.

When students take their turn, they will be listened to. There will be no attempt by anyone to manipulate what a student is offering. That is, the student will not be probed, interrupted, interpreted, analyzed, put-down, joked-at, advised, preached to, and so on. To "listen to" is to respectfully focus attention on the speaker and to let the speaker know that you have heard what he or she has said.

In the final analysis, the only way that a Sharing Circle can be evaluated is against these two criteria. Thus, if only two students choose to speak, but are listened to—even if they don't say very "deep" or "meaningful" things—the discussion group can be considered a success.

Training Student Leaders

A basic assumption of the Sharing Circle process is that every human being (barring those having considerable subnormal intelligence) has leadership potential. Further, the best time for energizing this ability is in childhood, and the optimum time for maintaining the skills is during adolescence. Students in countless elementary and secondary classrooms effectively lead their own circle sessions.

You can begin training student leaders after two or three successful circle sessions. Invite the students to consider volunteering to lead a Sharing Circle. Suggest that they watch you closely to see what steps the leader follows. At the end of the session, ask the students to describe what you did. They should be able to delineate the following steps:

The leader:

1. announces the topic and clarifies what it is about.

2. may lead a review of the Sharing Circle rules.

3. gives each person a turn who wants one.

4. asks discussion questions.

5. closes the circle.

Ask the students if anyone would like to volunteer to lead the next session. If no one volunteers, accept this outcome and wait for a session or two before trying again. If several volunteer, choose a student who you think is very likely to succeed. Then tell the group the topic you have in mind for the next session.

Before the next session, give the student leader a copy of the Sharing Circle, and discuss it with him or her. Also provide a copy of the Sharing Circle rules and Steps for Leading the Sharing Circle (see **"How to Lead a Sharing Circle"**). As the session begins, tell the group that you will be the trainer and speak about the process when necessary, but that otherwise, the student is the leader and you are a participant. Before turning the session over to the student leader add one more thing—a new ground rule stating that the students are expected to respect fully the leadership position of the student. **If they disagree with the student leader's procedure or are aware of what he or she should do next when the student leader may have forgotten, they are not to say anything at that time unless they are asked to by the student leader.** When people are learning a new skill, it can be very upsetting to have other people constantly reminding them of what they are supposed to do next. For this reason the student leader should not be heckled in any way. (Time can be taken at the end of the session for the group to give feedback and to thank the student leader for his or her performance).

Now, allow the student leader to proceed, interjecting statements yourself about the procedure only when absolutely necessary. Be sure to take your turn and model respectful listening. As necessary, deal with students who interrupt or distract the group.

Before ending the session, thank the student leader, and conduct a brief feedback session by asking the students,

"Who would like to tell (the student leader) what you liked about the way he or she conducted the session?" Let the student leader call on each person who has a comment.

Tell the students the topic you have in mind for the next session, and ask for a volunteer to lead it. Remember that students should not lead the group until you are sure they will be successful. Be careful to appoint leaders of both sexes and all racial/ethnic groups. Continue this process until all who wish to conduct a Sharing Circle are competent enough to lead them independently.

Combining Teacher, Counselor, and Student Leadership

This procedure allows several groups to meet simultaneously.

Begin by announcing to the class that you will be leading part of the Sharing Circle with the entire class and then they will break into their individual circles and complete them with students leading. If necessary, review the ground rules with the whole class. Then announce the topic, describe it and restate it. Finally, take your turn to relate to it personally. Answer any questions the students have, and then ask them to get into their groups.

When the circles are formed, the student leaders take over. They restate the topic and facilitate the sharing phase and, if desired, a review. The students return to their regular seating for the discussion question phase, which is led by the teacher or counselor.

Note: This is a particularly fruitful procedure if you are using Sharing Circles as supplements to your regular subject. The summary discussion can then include questions concerning the relevancy of the topic to subject matter currently being studied (see, **"Creating Your Own Sharing Circle Topics"**).

Creating Your Own Topics

Because Sharing Circles can be adapted to almost any situation and have such a wide range of positive outcomes, it is useful to understand the approach to creating them.

How Sharing Circle Topics Are Developed

Topics in the Sharing Circle program are presented according to a principle of learning that has been validated in a wide variety of applications. This principle is called successive approximation, and simply means, *begin where learners are or where they are likely to be and proceed to steps that are in keeping with the learners' progress*. The program is designed to help students develop useful insights into themselves and others while they practice positive communication skills. Circle session topics are experiential approximations of those insights.

Generally speaking, it is relatively easy to talk about things past and less easy to talk about right now. Second, it is typically easier to talk about other people and less easy to talk about oneself. Third, it seems to be easier for most people to talk about behavior than to talk about feelings. Finally, pleasant emotions are easier for most people to describe than negative ones. The examples that follow indicate topics at each end of the continuum for each of the four dimensions.

1. Past

"A Pleasant Memory"

Present

"Something I Feel Good About Today"

2. Other People

"Someone Did Something for Someone Else"

Self

"A Way I Take Care of Myself"

3. Behavior

"I Helped Someone Who Needed and Wanted My Help"

Feelings

"A Time I Felt Shy"

4. Positive Feelings

"Something That Makes Me Feel Good"

Negative Feelings

"Something That Makes Me Feel Sad"

Thoughts on Developing Your Own Topics

Many teachers and students generate topics tailor-made to fit their needs. If these topics are generated so that the less complex are presented first, moving sequentially toward the more complex, the principle of learning underlying the program will be maintained. Insights may come anywhere along the continuum, but they are more likely to occur when students are on familiar ground. The test of ease for a topic will be the sharing in the circle. Here are three other points to keep in mind:

1. **If you create a topic that relates to an issue of some kind, remember that in issue-oriented Sharing Circles there need be no agreement.** The Sharing Circle is not a rap session. Each person merely voices his or her own thoughts and feelings about the issue. The emphasis is on listening to one another's remarks and becoming aware of one's own thoughts and feelings. During the summary discussion, elicit comments from the students on the similarities and differences in their feelings and thoughts and ask open-ended, thought-provoking questions.

2. **Do not initiate a topic that might be a lead-in for ax-grinding on the part of you or anyone else in the circle.** If you need to express strong feelings to the students, find another method. The same principle applies to a situation in which one or more students have some strong feelings to express to each other. *The Sharing Circle is not a setting for confrontation, not even subtle confrontation!*

Guidelines for Developing Sharing Circle Topics

Formulate topics in light of the considerations already mentioned. To avoid the repetitious "A Time...," other starters for topics are:

"When..."	"An Idea I..."
"One of..."	"The Way..."
"Something I..."	"How..."
"What..."	"Things I..."
"One Way..."	"The Thing That..."

Consider what you are trying to achieve with the topic. Does it relate to one of the three growth areas, Awareness, Personal Mastery, or Interpersonal Skills? Is it in harmony with other aspects of your curriculum?

Be sure to present the topic to the students in an open-ended manner. Elaborate on it. Mention suggestions and possibilities to help them start thinking about it. State the topic at the beginning of your introduction and again at the end.

As you listen to students respond, do not feel compelled to question them. If you do ask a question, be sure it's open-ended and asked with the intention of helping them express themselves more fully. In general, questions asked to students when they are sharing should help students develop an awareness of **feelings**, their own and others. For example:

— Do you remember how you felt at the time?
— How do you feel about that now?

Questions may enable students to become more aware of their **behavior**.

— Do you remember what you said/did when it happened?
— How did other people act/react in that situation?

Questions may help students focus on their own **thoughts**, including attitudes, beliefs, preferences, etc., to learn more about how their thoughts influence their feelings and behavior.

— Did any thought or image cross your mind when that happened?
— Do you remember how that idea caused you to feel or act?

Guidelines for Developing Discussion Questions.

The purpose of the discussion questions is to involve students intellectually, to encourage them to examine the implications of what they have shared, and to stimulate higher-order thinking skills.

The summary starters listed to the right relate to Awareness, Personal Mastery, and Interpersonal Skills.

Awareness

— What kinds of things do people do...?
— If you feel...does that mean...?
— What is it that...?
— What kinds of things do...?
— When people...?
— If you want..., then...?

Personal Mastery

— How can a person...?
— Do you think...should have to...?
— What can you do when...?
— Is it too early/late to...?

Interpersonal Skills

— If you want people to..., then...?
— Would all of us...?
— Are there ways we...?
— Are there times when...?
— What can you say to...?

101 Life-Skills Topics

What I Think Good Communication Is

Objective:

The students will describe the role of effective communication in relating to other people.

Introduce the Topic:

Say to the students: *Our topic for this circle session is "What I Think Good Communication Is." Almost all of the contact we have with other people involves communicating in one way or another. Sometimes this communication is in writing and other times it involves speaking and listening. Did you know that a good deal of our communication involves body language? We call this non-verbal communication. Think of the things we must do to be good communicators. Take a moment and think about how you would describe truly good communication. Think about what good communication means to all of the people involved in your example, and describe that, too. When you are ready, we can begin to discuss our topic, which is, "What I Think Good Communication Is."*

Discussion Questions:

When all the students who wish to have shared, ask a number of open-ended questions to encourage a discussion:
1. *What are some of the results of good communication?*
2. *What can happen when communication is NOT good?*
3. *How does it feel when you know that communication between you and another person is good? ...is poor?*

A Way I Let Others Know I'm Interested In What They Say

Objective:

The students will describe specific ways they behave when listening to others that convey their interest in what is being discussed.

Introduce the Topic:

Say to the students: *Our topic for this session is, "A Way I Let Others Know I'm Interested in What They Say." One way we can let another person know that we are listening and interested in what they have to say is by what we say in response. There are many other things we can do, too. Some of these involve our posture, the way we make eye contact, or whether or how frequently we interrupt them. Think of some of the ways you show other people that you are interested in what they are saying. Also think about how you feel when others listen to you with interest. Select one of the ways you show interest and tell us about it, if you'd like. Our topic is, "A Way I Let Others Know I'm Interested in What They Say."*

Discussion Questions:

1. *How do you think people feel knowing that you are really interested in what they have to say?*
2. *How do you feel knowing that others are interested in what you have to say?*
3. *What things can a person do to become a more effective listener or communicator?*

A Time When I Really Felt Heard

Objectives:

The students will:
—describe the importance of listening in the communication process.
—describe feelings generated by being recognized and heard.

Introduce the Topic:

Say to the students: *Today our topic is, "A Time I Really Felt Heard." We know that attention is a universal need. Sometimes we do not get it for one reason or another, but when we do our feelings are generally positive.*

Think of a time when you really needed to be heard and someone listened to you. Perhaps you had some kind of a problem that you wanted to talk out, or maybe you had an experience that you wanted to tell someone about. Who listened to you? How did you feel after you had expressed yourself? Think about it for a few moments. The topic is, "A Time When I Really Felt Heard."

Discussion Questions:

1. *How are people generally affected when their feelings are not accepted?*
2. *Do people keep their feelings to themselves because they think they won't be accepted?*
3. *When people risk saying how they feel, do others respect them for it? Do you? Why or why not?*
4. *How did you feel about the person who listened to you?*
5. *How did you feel about yourself?*
6. *What happens to communication when people don't listen well?*

Once When Somebody Wouldn't Listen to Me

Objectives:

The students will:
—describe the importance of listening in the communication process.
—make verbal distinctions between attentive, conscious listening and inattentive, unconscious hearing.
—describe the need of people for attention and the consequences of not receiving it.

Introduce the Topic:

Say to the students: *Today we're going to talk about a common frustration that occurs in the communication process. Our topic is "Once When Someone Wouldn't Listen to Me."*

Did you ever need to have someone listen to you who wouldn't? Maybe the person you were talking to didn't agree with what you were saying and refused to listen. Or perhaps he or she was busy and didn't want to be bothered. How did you feel? You've probably noticed your little brother or sister, or seen a pet, like your dog or cat, trying to get someone's attention. People and animals can feel lost when they don't get needed attention, and it's especially important for people to be listened to when they need to talk about something. Take a minute to thing about it, and tell us about a time when you had an experience like this. The topic is "Once When Someone Wouldn't Listen to Me."

Discussion Questions:

1. What similarities and differences did you notice in our feelings about not being listened to?
2. What can you do when you're not being listened to?
3. Should a person expect to be listened to every time he or she has something to say? Why or why not?
4. How did you feel when you are being ignored?

How I Got Someone to Pay Attention to Me

Objectives:

The students will:
—verbalize the importance of receiving interpersonal attention.
—state the importance of paying attention as a skill.
—identify positive, effective strategies for getting attention.

Introduce the Title:

Say to the students: *Our topic for this session is "How I Got Someone to Pay Attention to Me." When you or I want to communicate with someone, first of all we have to get the person to notice us. We have to do something to get the other person to focus on us. As you have probably noticed, there are many ways to do this. You can do something funny, helpful, destructive, informative, exciting, or whatever, and people will automatically look at you.*

You are invited to share a time when you got someone's attention in a particular situation. Perhaps you tried to get the attention of a person who was a long way away from you in a large crowd. Or perhaps the person whose attention you were trying to get was watching TV or doing something else nearby. Think about it for a few moments. The topic is, "How I Got Someone to Pay Attention to Me."

Discussion Questions:

1. *Do people really need attention?*
2. *Does the way you get attention have anything at all to do with the kind of attention you get or how long the attention lasts?*
3. *What do you think a person would be like who never got any attention?*
4. *What does giving your attention have to do with good communication?*
5. *What did the other person seem to think of your attention-getting method?*

My Greatest Strength

Objectives:

The students will:
—Identify a personal strength, ability, or talent.
—Discuss the difficulties and benefits of making positive statements about themselves.

Introduce the Topic:

Our topic today is, "My Greatest Strength." We all have strengths and abilities that cause us to experience positive feelings. Today, I'd like you to choose the one that you think is your greatest — one that makes you feel very proud. Maybe you have musical or artistic talent, make friends easily, are good at leading others, or have a terrific sense of humor. Or maybe you have developed a lot of skill in a particular sport, cook delicious meals at home, or are a whiz in science or math. It's hard to talk about these things sometimes, because it feels like we're boasting. But in this session you have permission to boast. Think this over for a minute and, if you will, tell us your thoughts. The topic is, "My Greatest Strength."

Discussion Questions:

1. How do you feel when talking about your strengths?
2. Why is it hard for lots of people to say positive things about themselves?
3. What benefits are there in stating your strengths?

An Ability or Talent I'm Proud Of

Objectives:

The students will:
—describe an ability or talent.
—discuss the importance of acknowledging one's own strengths and abilities.
—demonstrate appreciation for the abilities of others.

Introduce the Topic:

Say to the students: *This is going to be an unusual circle session because we are going to encourage each other to do something most people don't do very often. We're going to take credit for things we're good at. Most of the time people are modest, but today we will ignore any rules of modesty we've learned, which will probably do us good. The topic is, "An Ability or Talent I'm Proud Of."*

It's obvious that everyone has strengths and weaknesses. No one is good at everything and no one is poor at everything. Think for a minute about those things at which you are just naturally good. Think about your special skills. Maybe you excel in an academic area like Math, Science, or English. Or perhaps you have an athletic skill you're proud of. Maybe you have artistic talents, or are good at making things with your hands. You might have inherited your abilities from your parents, or you may be the only one in your family who has them. Think it over for a few moments. The topic is, "An Ability or Talent I'm Proud Of."

Discussion Questions:

1. How did we feel telling each other about our abilities and talents? Did it feel a bit like bragging?
2. What benefits do we get from talking about our strengths and abilities?
3. How did you feel about each other during this session?
4. How did you develop your strengths and abilities?

One of the Nicest Things That Ever Happened to Me

Objectives:

The students will:
—recall and relate a favorite memory.
—identify some of the benefits of reliving past events.

Introduce the Topic:

Our topic for this session is, "One of the Nicest Things That Ever Happened to Me." Take a moment to think about some of your most treasured memories and choose one to concentrate on. Your memory could be of something that happened as recently as today, or it could be something from your childhood. It might involve a special event, like a birthday, holiday, or vacation. Or perhaps your pleasant memory is of a person, a pet, or funny incident. Close you eyes and try to remember everything about the event: the surroundings, what happened, any special smells, tastes, shapes, textures, colors, patterns, or other things that make the memory more vivid. Then tell us what happened and what your feelings were. The topic is, "One of the Nicest Things That Ever Happened to Me."

Discussion Questions:

1. *To what extent did your memory bring back thoughts about the event, and to what extent did you actually relive the emotions involved?*
2. *What are some of the ways that we hold on to pleasant memories?*
3. *What are the benefits of reliving of favorite memories?*

A Special Occasion or Holiday That Relates to My Culture

Objectives:

The students will:

—describe a traditional event that they observe and explain its significance.

—discuss the role of tradition in life and explain how they benefit from honoring their cultural traditions.

Introduce the Topic:

In today's circle, we're going to talk about something that belongs to your culture or cultural heritage. The topic is, "A Special Occasion or Holiday That Relates to My Culture." Some special occasions are referred to in English as "rites of passage." Events like the christening of a baby, a baptism, bat/bar mitzvah, wedding, or funeral mark a person's passage from one stage in life to another. Not every event of this nature is enjoyable, of course, but even funerals offer a kind of comfort to family members.

Many of the values and attitudes handed down from one generation to another last a long time because they are a traditional part of a certain way of life; they stand for something treasured. Examples are the Fourth of July, Cinco de Mayo, Halloween, Easter, or Passover. Take a moment to think of a special occasion that relates to your culture — a rite of passage or a holiday — that you particularly enjoy and appreciate. The topic is, "A Special Occasion or Holiday That Relates to My Culture."

Discussion Questions:

1. What do holidays and rites of passage do for people?
2. Why is it important to honor cultural traditions?
3. How do you feel about doing traditional things that your ancestors did?

Something I Like That Is Part of Another Culture

Objectives:

The students will:
—name a favorite contribution that some other culture makes to their life.
—describe the benefits of living in a culturally diverse nation.

Introduce the Topic:

In today's session, we are going to focus on things we appreciate that are part of a culture other than our own. The topic is, "Something I Like That Is Part of Another Culture." Maybe you appreciate a type of music or dance that originated in another culture. Perhaps you like the sound of German, the paintings and murals of Mexican artists, or the spiritual traditions of Native Americans. What kinds of ethnic foods do you enjoy? Basque? Greek? Thai? Chinese? French? There are lots of businesses in our country that thrive by making things from other countries available to people in this country. If you'd like to share, describe the thing that impresses you and tell about any special feelings that go along with it. The topic is, "Something I Like That Is Part of Another Culture."

Discussion Questions:

1. What similarities did you notice in the things we shared?
2. If something from your culture or cultural heritage was mentioned, how did that cause you to feel?
3. What are some of the many ways we benefit by living in a culturally diverse nation?

My Favorite Subject at School

Objectives:

The students will:
—identify personal strengths in academic areas.
—describe what they like about their favorite school subject.

Introduce the Topic.

In your own words, say to the students: *Today we're going to talk about what we most like to study. The topic is, "My Favorite Subject at School." Do you have a favorite subject at school? Is it one that is easier for you than others—one in which you get good grades? Or is it a subject that you don't know a lot about yet, but are eager to learn? Maybe your favorite subject changes each year; then again, maybe you always seem to prefer the same one. Tell us what you like about the subject, and how you feel about yourself when you are learning it. Does your favorite subject have anything to do with what you might want to be when you grow up? Think about it silently for a minute, and then we will begin to share. The topic is, "My Favorite Subject at School."*

Discussion Questions:

1. *What are some of the thoughts and feelings we have about our favorite subjects?*
2. *How do you think your favorite subject will help you become what you want to be in the future?*
3. *Why are some subjects favored over others?*

My Favorite Hero or Heroine

Objectives:

The students will:
—identify a person or character whom they see as heroic.
—describe how the accomplishments of their hero relate to their own needs as individuals.

**Introduce
the Topic:**

The topic today is, "My Favorite Hero or Heroine." Think about real-life people and fictional characters whom you see as heroes and heroines.

Does a real person come to your mind? It might be someone you know personally, such as a member of your family. Or it might be someone whom you know of, like a politician or an entertainer. This hero or heroine might also be someone who is no longer alive, such as a figure from history whom you admire. He or she might even be a fictional character from a movie, TV show, book, or play. Take a minute to think about it. Then, tell us who your favorite fictional or real-life hero or heroine is and what you like and admire about this person. The topic is, "My Favorite Hero or Heroine."

**Discussion
Questions:**

1. What similarities and differences did you notice in the people we think of as heroes and heroines?
2. Why do people need to have heroes and heroines?
3. What does your hero or heroine tell you about your own needs, wants, dreams, or goals?

My Favorite Villain

Objectives:

The students will:
—identify a person or fictional character whom they consider villainous and describe the person's traits.
—explain what their choice of a villain implies about their own values and beliefs.

Introduce the topic:

Our topic for this session may strike you as being kind of funny at first. It is, "My Favorite Villain." Think about an individual, either real or fictional, whom you consider to be a villain. You might choose someone from literature, like Captain Hook or The Big Bad Wolf, or you might choose a real person who has done something that you consider villainous, like Adolph Hitler. This is a person you almost enjoy disliking or hating. Tell us who the person is and why you dislike him or her. However, if the person you have in mind is someone we know personally, please don't use his or her name. Our topic is, "My Favorite Villain."

Discussion Questions:

1. Did you notice any similarities in the people or characters we chose as villains?
2. What do we gain by creating villainous characters in movies and books?
3. What do you learn about yourself when you examine the character of your villain?

Someone I'd Like to Be Like

Objectives:

The students will:

—identify a role model and describe the influence that person has on their life.

—discuss how and why they choose certain role models.

Introduce the Topic:

Our topic for this session is, "Someone I'd like to Be Like." You've all heard the term "model." When you hear it, you probably think of a photographer's model or a fashion model. Or maybe you think of a model airplane, car, or train. There's another meaning for the word model. It means anyone who shows you how to act or how to do something. Parents and teachers are models for children, and so are you. You show them how to be teenagers.

This session offers us a chance to talk about our own models. Do you know an older teenager, a young adult, or an older adult whom you look up to? This is someone you probably find yourself imitating. It might be someone you know personally, like an older brother, sister, cousin, or neighbor. Or it might be someone you don't know personally, like a TV star or a political figure. Think about it for a minute. Then tell us about a person who is a model for you. The topic is, "Someone I'd Like to Be Like."

Discussion Questions:

1. What characteristics did our models have in common?

2. What causes you to choose one role model and not another?

3. Is it possible to learn how not to be from certain models? Explain.

Something I Like to Imagine

Objective:

The students will discuss their feelings and behavior by focusing first on their creative thoughts.

Introduce the Topic:

Say to the students: *Our topic for this session is "Something I Like to Imagine." Did you know that using your imagination is a very healthy and important thing to do? You may find yourself daydreaming and not realize that what you're doing is necessary. You need to daydream and imagine things, even if what you are imaging seems absurd or ridiculous. So think about something you like to imagine. Maybe it's reliving an event from the past or imaging what it would be like to experience something you've never done. Perhaps it's a wish or a creative idea concerning something you'd like to make or write about. Or it could be a wild fantasy of some kind. Whatever it is, we would like to hear about it. The topic is, "Something I Like to Imagine."*

Discussion Questions:

After the students have finished sharing, ask several open-ended questions to spark a discussion:
1. *In what ways do you think daydreaming and using your imagination help you to be creative?*
2. *What do you think people would be like if they had no powers of imagination?*
3. *Did you learn something about someone in this session that you didn't know before?*
4. *What feelings do you experience when you imagine the thing you shared?*

One of My Favorite Pastimes

Objectives:

The students will:
—describe a leisure activity they enjoy.
—describe the importance of leisure.
—discuss how interests and activities are expressions of uniqueness.

Introduce the Topic:

Say to the students: *Our circle session topic today is, "One of My Favorite Pastimes." A pastime, of course, is a way you like to "pass" or spend time. In other words, what do you like to do when there is no pressure on you to do anything? What do you prefer to do when the choice is entirely yours?*

Perhaps you are an energetic person and you enjoy sports or games so, whenever you get a chance, you get together with friends and engage in those activities. Maybe you prefer artistic endeavors, like painting, music, or dance. Or perhaps your favorite pastime is just relaxing—reading, watching T.V., or spending time with friends or family. Think it over and tell us what you enjoy doing. The topic is, "One of My Favorite Pastimes."

Discussion Questions:

1. Did you notice any similarities in the pastimes we mentioned and why we enjoy them?
2. Were there any interesting differences? What pastimes were mentioned by only one person?
3. Why is it important to have leisure? ...leisure activities?

Something I Enjoy Doing That I Do Well

Objective:

The students will share positive things about themselves with one another.

Introduce the Topic:

Say to the students: *In this session, we are going to talk about things we like to do and brag a little bit in the process. The topic is "Something I Enjoy Doing That I Do Well." So take a moment to think about something that you are good at, that you would feel OK telling the group about. Perhaps it's something you do away from school that none of us could know about unless you told us, or it could be something you are accomplishing in one of your classes. Tell us about anything that you like to do and do well.*

Don't be bashful about admitting that you do something well, because we already know that you've got talents and abilities. Everyone does. In this session, you have permission to talk about them. Think for a moment, If you don't feel like talking, just listen; that's fine, too. The topic is "Something I Enjoy Doing That I Do Well."

Discussion Questions:

After the students have finished sharing, encourage them to talk about what they learned. Ask these and other questions:
1. *How did you feel about describing what you do well?*
2. *Do you think it's OK to do things just for fun, or should everything we do be productive?*
3. *Did you learn anything that you didn't know before about someone in the circle?*

A Favorite Place of Mine

Objectives:

The students will:
—describe a place they enjoy being.
—discuss how preferences make each person unique.

**Introduce
the Topic:**

Say to the students: *Our topic for this circle session is a
very enjoyable one because it encourages us to talk about
ourselves and the things we like. The topic is, "A Favorite
Place of Mine." So give that some thought.*

*Where do you really enjoy being? Perhaps an exciting
place comes to mind, or one that's peaceful and beautiful.
Maybe the most important thing about a place is who is
there with you. Or perhaps when you think of a favorite
place you usually focus on feeling relaxed or inspired. The
place that comes to mind might be one you've seen in a
picture or movie, but haven't yet visited. It might even be
an imaginary place. Think about it for a few moments.
The topic is, "A Favorite Place of Mine."*

**Discussion
Questions:**

1. *Did you notice any similarities in the places we
   mentioned and why we like those places?*
2. *How do your surroundings affect your mood? ...your
   thoughts?*
3. *Why do we depend on familiar surroundings?*
4. *What kind of person regularly seeks new and different
   surroundings?*

A Time I Won and Loved It

Objectives:

The students will:

—describe a victorious experience and the good feelings that went with it.

—state that there do not always have to be losers in order for someone to win.

—identify circumstances under which everyone can be a winner.

Introduce the Topic:

The topic for this session is, "A Time I Won and Loved It." Each of us has had the experience of winning, of tasting victory, of overcoming difficult situations. Think of a time when you did something that caused you to feel like a winner! Maybe you won a game or athletic contest, or perhaps you showed a lot of courage and accomplished something that made you feel very proud. Maybe you won a prize or an award, were elected to a class office, or got the highest grade on a test. Take a minute to think about a time when you were the winner and felt wonderful about it. The topic is, "A Time I Won and Loved It."

Discussion Questions:

1. *What kinds of feelings do you have when you win?*
2. *Do other people have to lose in order for you to feel like a winner? Why or why not?*
3. *What are some situations in which everyone can be a winner?*

A Time I Lost and Took It Hard

Objectives:

The students will:
—describe a time when they lost at something.
—discuss the dynamics of losing and why losing is so difficult.
—name situations in which everyone can be a winner.

Introduce the Topic:

Our topic for this session is, "A Time I Lost and Took It Hard." Maybe you'll have to think about this one a little bit, or possibly something has already popped into your head. Think of a time when you wanted very much to win at something. You may have worked hard at it, and put all your hopes into it, but you lost. And you felt very badly.

Maybe you tried out for a play, a team, or a cheerleading squad. Or maybe you studied hard for a test and thought you had all the answers. Maybe you entered a contest or a race for a class office, but somebody else won instead of you. You may tell us about something that happened recently or a long time ago. Take a minute to think about it and, if you will, tell us about, "A Time I Lost and Took It Hard."

Discussion Questions:

1. *What makes certain losses particularly difficult to take?*
2. *When does winning become too important to people?*
3. *Do there always have to be losers in order to have winners, or can you think of situations in which everybody wins*

A Skill or Talent of Mine that I Could Use in a Job

Objectives:

The students will:
—assess personal aptitudes, interests, and abilities relative to career possibilities.
—apply skills to plan or revise a career plan.

Introduce the Topic:

Say to the students: *Our topic for this session is, "A Skill or Talent of Mine that I Could Use in a Job." We all have skills and talents that we use every day. Some of these skills and talents are important not only to students, but to employees in many different jobs. Perhaps you work well with people. Or maybe your strongest talent lies in dealing with information. Maybe you make friends easily, or handle confrontations tactfully and diplomatically. Perhaps you are good at solving math problems, or organizing materials. Do you like to build or repair things? Do you draw, sing, play a musical instrument, or dance well? All of these skills and talents are useful in certain jobs. Some are useful in many jobs. Tell us about a talent or skill you have and how you could use it in a job. Think it over for a few moments. The topic is, "A Skill or Talent of Mine that I Could Use in a Job."*

Discussion Questions:

1. *Which skills and talents were mentioned most often?*
2. *Which skills and talents are needed in almost every kind of job?*
3. *How can knowledge of your skills and talents assist you in planning a career direction?*

A Job I Would Really Enjoy

Objectives:

The students will:
—describe a job they would enjoy doing.
—demonstrate positive attitudes toward work and learning.
—relate educational achievement to career opportunities.
—relate careers to the needs and functions of the economy and society.

Introduce the Topic:

Say to the students: *Our topic for this session is, "A Job I Would Really Enjoy." There are probably many jobs you would enjoy doing. Think of one, and tell us why it appeals to you. Maybe you know you would like to be a park ranger because you love the outdoors and are interested in conservation. Perhaps you're certain you would enjoy being a robotics engineer because you have already successfully built three robots. Maybe you are fascinated with the structure of cities, so you think you would enjoy being a city planner, an architect, or an urban geographer. Maybe independence or travel are your top priorities, so you think you would enjoy being a travel writer. Perhaps you want to contribute to society by developing new sources of energy, so you hope to become a physicist. Think about it for a few moments and then tell us what job you would enjoy and why. The topic is, "One Job I Would Really Enjoy."*

Discussion Questions:

1. *What similarities and differences were there among the things we shared?*
2. *Which of the jobs mentioned would require education beyond high school?*
3. *How did some of the jobs mentioned meet an important need of society?*
4. *What skills would be needed in all of the jobs that were mentioned?*

A Job I Think I Would Dislike

Objective:

The students will identify a job or career they don't want to pursue, and describe why it is wrong for them.

Introduce the Topic:

Say to the students: *Our topic for this session is, "A Job I Think I Would Dislike." We all want to be happy in our jobs. Consequently, we develop opinions about jobs that we think would <u>not</u> make us happy, jobs we would dislike. Can you think of a job you're almost positive you wouldn't want to have? Maybe you wouldn't want to be an accountant because to you the job sounds boring and repetitive, and you would have to work at a desk all day. Perhaps you wouldn't want to be a management consultant because you would have to travel a great deal, and continually work with strangers. Maybe the job of construction worker is not for you because it can be dirty and physically challenging. Maybe you would turn down the opportunity to become a nurse because nursing is a relatively low-paying profession. Take a few moments to think about it. The topic is, "A Job I Think I Would Dislike."*

Discussion Questions:

1. *What is the major difference between the job you dislike and one you like?*
2. *How were our dislikes similar? How were they different?*
3. *How essential to the economy is the job you dislike? How essential is it to society?*
4. *What would it take to make you like the job you described?*

A Time I Remember Feeling Totally Alive and in Touch With the World

Objectives:

The students will:
—recall and relate a peak experience.
—discuss how the mind and emotions affect body
sensations and feelings of physical well-being.

Introduce the Topic:

Our topic for this session is, "A Time I Remember Feeling Totally Alive and in Touch With the World." Let's think of, and reexperience, times in our lives when we felt really, really good. These kinds of experiences are sometimes called "peak experiences."

Perhaps you remember being in a special place and feeling full of joy and energy. Maybe you felt wonderfully well because of the person or people you were with. Or maybe you experienced these feelings because you had just accomplished something significant, or were looking forward with joyful anticipation to a long-awaited trip or special event. You can tell us about a childhood experience, or a recent event. Our topic is, "A Time I Remember Feeling Totally Alive and in Touch With the World."

Discussion Questions:

1. What similarities did you notice in the things we shared?
2. How did your body feel during the moments you described?
3. What does that tell you about the connection between your mind and your body?

A Feeling of Sadness I Remember

Objectives:

The students will:
—tell about an experience that caused them sadness or grief.
—identify sadness and grief as normal emotions.
—name positive ways of handling feelings of sadness.

Introduce the Topic:

Our topic for this session is, "A Feeling of Sadness I Remember." We all feel sad at times. Life definitely has a negative as well as positive side, and if we didn't experience the negative, we couldn't fully enjoy the positive.

Can you remember a time when you felt sadness or grief about something? Maybe you lost a loved one, or a pet. Perhaps you had to move to a new neighborhood or city and leave good friends behind. Or maybe you experienced a great disappointment, like losing a critical game, not being accepted for a program or job you wanted, or being rejected by someone you cared for. Let's take a minute to think of times we've experienced sadness. The topic is, "A Feeling of Sadness I Remember."

Discussion Questions:

1. *What similarities did you notice in the experiences we shared?*
2. *Since sadness is a normal emotion, why do we try so hard to avoid it?*
3. *How do you help yourself when you feel sad?*

A Time I Was Alone, But Not Lonely

Objectives:

The students will:
—distinguish between being alone and feeling lonely.
—describe the benefits of finding time to be alone.
—identify ways of handling feelings of loneliness.

Introduce the Topic:

Our topic for this session is, "A Time I Was Alone, But Not Lonely." Being alone and feeling lonely are not always the same thing. Sometimes it's nice to get away and be with ourselves. We can relax, rest our minds, and think about whatever we want. In the company of just yourself, you can achieve greater self-understanding and appreciation.

Try to remember a time when you were alone and had a good feeling about it. Maybe you took a walk by yourself, or spent an afternoon alone at home reading and thinking, or sat under a tree at the park and did nothing. You may have experienced a lot of feelings, but loneliness was not one of them. Tell us what you did feel, and what you learned from the experience. The topic is, "A Time I Was Alone, But Not Lonely."

Discussion Questions:

1. What is the difference between being alone and being lonely?
2. How do you arrange for "alone time" when you need it?
3. How can you make yourself feel better when you are experiencing loneliness?

A Time I Felt Scared

Objectives:

The students will:
—describe experiences that caused them to feel fear.
—state that fear is a normal emotion.

Introduce the Topic:

State the topic. Say: *Everyone feels scared from time to time and no one likes the feeling. Today, we are going to talk about feeling afraid. The topic is, "A Time I Felt Scared."*

Can you think of a time that you were afraid? What happened to cause your fear? Were you lost? Were you around a lot of people that you didn't know? Was it the first day of school? Perhaps you felt afraid the first time you tried to swim in a pool or the ocean. Chances are there is something that makes you feel scared even now. Are you afraid of the dark? Do big dogs frighten you? Maybe you feel scared when Mommy and Daddy have an argument and yell. Close your eyes and think of one time when you felt afraid. When you look up, I'll know that you are ready to begin the sharing circle. The topic is, "A Time I Felt Scared."

Discussion Questions:

1. How do we feel inside when we are scared?
2. What do we sometimes do when we are afraid?
3. Why is it important to talk about our fears?
4. How can we help each other handle our fears?

How My Fear Helped Me Realize a Danger

Objectives:

The students will:
—describe how fear alerted them to possible danger.
—explore the function of fear as a valid warning signal.

Introduce the Topic:

Our topic for this session is, "How My Fear Helped Me Realize a Danger." Feelings of fear are meant to protect us from getting hurt or killed. Sometimes fear follows a thought, such as, "Hmmm, that dog looks mean." Sometimes fear comes unannounced — you just start feeling uneasy. In cases like this, the fear may be based on a subconscious awareness. Everyone experiences fear at one time or another. Reasonable fear makes sense and is very useful in our lives.

Can you remember a time when you were scared, and it turned out that your fear had a real purpose? Maybe you were home alone at night, and fear reminded you to lock all the doors and windows. Perhaps you saw a car coming and something about its approach caused you to move aside, only to find out later that it had caused a crash. Does a fear of high places make you cautious near the edge of a cliff or roof? Has fear ever alerted you to danger when a stranger approached you on the street or at the park? Think about it for a few moments. The topic is, "How My Fear Helped Me Realize a Danger."

Discussion Questions:

1. Why do you think people sometimes tell each other not to be afraid or tease each other for getting scared?
2. When is fear unreasonable?
3. Why do people like to attend movies that frighten them?

I Felt Good and Bad About the Same Thing

Objectives:

The students will:
—Describe an incident in which they experienced conflicting emotions.
—state that conflicting feelings are common and natural.

Introduce the Topic:

Today our topic is, "I Felt Good and Bad About the Same Thing." You've probably noticed that hardly anything seems to be all good or all bad. Even things that are wonderful and marvelous are hardly ever perfect, and things that seem dreadful may have one or two positive features. Even our worst mistakes can be good things if we learn something important from them.

Can you think of a time when you had mixed feelings about something? For example, maybe you went to the dentist with a toothache. You anticipated that whatever the dentist did would bring you relief — a good feeling — but you were scared that it might be painful — a bad feeling. You might remember mixed feelings associated with special events, friendships, work, decisions — just about anything. Think about it for a moment, and tell us something that caused you to feel both bad and good. The topic is, "I Felt Good and Bad About the Same Thing."

Discussion Questions:

1. Why do we sometimes have conflicting emotions?
2. When your feelings conflict, which ones do you tend to show? Why?
3. What did you learn about feelings from this session?

A Place Where I Feel Safe

Objectives:

The students will:
—describe the features of a setting in which they feel safe.
—identify components of a secure, trust-building environment.

Introduce the Topic:

Our topic for this session is, "A Place Where I Feel Safe." We have all experienced the feeling of being in a place where we feel good. Often, one of the main reasons we feel good is that, for some personal reason, the environment feels safe. Can you think of a place where you almost always experience a feeling of safety? Maybe you feel safe in your home, or almost anywhere provided you are in the company of a particular person. Perhaps you feel safe when you are with a certain group of friends, or tucked under a the covers of your own bed. The safety you feel may come from the place itself, or the person or people, you are with. Take a minute to examine your own experiences and see if there's a place like this for you. The topic is, "A Place Where I Feel Safe."

Discussion Questions:

1. What features or qualities does this place have that cause you to feel safe?
2. What features or qualities would make a place unsafe for you?
3. Does the circle feel like a safe place? Why or why not?
4. Why is one's environment such a factor in determining emotional and psychological well being?

When My Body Felt Tired But Good at the Same Time

Objective:

The students will:
—describe a positive experience involving exercise.
—explore positive feelings associated with physical labor, exercise, and exertion.

Introduce the Topic:

Today our topic is, "When My Body Felt Tired But Good at the Same Time." One of the ways people become fit is through physical exercise. Another is through physical labor. Of course, we've all had times when we've really overdone this, and our aching bodies bore testimony to too much, too soon! But whether or not you were in shape, you've probably had the experience of exerting yourself and then having a good feeling — a feeling that you earned your pleasure with every strain of your muscles. Maybe you cleaned out the attic, jogged several miles, played a game of basketball with some friends, weeded a garden, lifted a lot of heavy machinery, or danced at a party until you thought your legs were going to fall off. See if you can remember a time like this. The topic is, "When My Body Felt Tired But Good at the Same Time."

Discussion Questions:

1. Why do you think physical exercise is so important to feeling healthy and in good spirits?
2. Many people report that while their bodies are working, their minds get a change of pace. Do you believe that minds need a change of pace?
3. What is the relationship between our bodies and our minds and emotions?

Some of the Best Health/Appearance Advice I Ever Heard

Objective:

The students will describe a health practice they value and observe.

Introduce the Topic:

Say to the students: *Most of us feel kind of excited when someone shares a secret with us, and today we're going to do that in our circle session. The secrets we share will have to do with becoming very healthy, strong, and great looking and staying that way. The topic is, "Some of the Best Health/Appearance Advice I Ever Heard."*

No doubt you've heard lots of health tips, as well as advice for improving your appearance, and maybe you've followed some of those ideas and found they worked. Think of some advice that you were given by another person, and successfully tried. The person could have been anyone—a doctor, dentist, coach, teacher, parent, or friend. What the person suggested could have been an important, but often forgotten, bit of common sense like the value of flossing your teeth once a day. Or maybe it was something rather exotic like doing Hatha Yoga to improve muscle tone and acquire a sense of inner peace. Think it over. The topic is, "Some of the Best Health/Appearance Advice I Ever Heard."

Discussion Questions:

1. Who are the best people to give us good advice regarding health and appearance?
2. What ideas did you hear that seem worth trying?
3. Why don't all ideas work equally well for everyone?
4. Why are some people more interested in their health than others? ...in their appearance?

Something That Causes Me Stress

Objective:

The students will:
—describe causes of personal stress.
—discuss specific things that can be done to relieve stress.
—state that feelings of stress are normal.

Introduce the Topic:

Say to the students: *Our topic for this session is, "Something That Causes Me Stress." Do you ever get tongue tied? Feel uptight or on edge? Get a headache or a queezie stomach when you're not sick? Chances are the cause of those feelings is stress. Many different things can cause stress— worrying about a test, feeling angry at someone, or not getting enough sleep, for example. Even good things can cause stress—like the excitement of waiting for a special event. Think of something that causes you stress and tell us about it. What happens to cause the stress, and how does it affect the way you feel, the thoughts you have, and the things you do? Take a few minutes to think about it. The topic is, "Something That Causes Me Stress."*

Discussion Questions:

1. Why do people experience stress?
2. Do the same kinds of things frequently cause you stress?
3. If you know something is likely to stress you, what can you do about it?
4. Do feelings of stress do us any good? Explain your answer.

Something I Worried About That Turned Out OK

Objectives:

The students will:
—describe a time they worried about something.
—describe ways in which worry can inhibit normal functioning.
—identify ways of avoiding unnecessary worry.

Introduce the Topic:

Say to the students: *Our topic for this session is "Something I Worried About That Turned Out OK." There are many things in our lives that cause us to become concerned. When we are concerned about something, we usually focus our attention on whatever it is until we are no longer concerned. Sometimes our concern becomes so great that it changes into worry. When we are worried about something, we may find it hard to think about other things that are going on in our lives. When this happens, worry is getting in the way of our leading a normal and productive life. It is producing serious stress.*

Think about something that you have experienced in your life that has worried you very much. It may be something that happened recently or perhaps it occurred many years ago. It doesn't need to be something really big and important. In fact, when we look back on the things about which we worried in the past, they sometimes appear to be insignificant. Whatever it is you choose to share, we'd like to hear about it. The topic is, "Something I Worried About That Turned Out OK."

Discussion Questions:

1. *How does your body react when you're worried?*
2. *What kinds of feelings do you have when you are no longer worried about something, or find that it wasn't worth your worry?*
3. *In what ways can over-worry harm us or get in our way?*
4. *How often do we worry about things unnecessarily?*

Something I Do for My Own Well-Being

Objectives:

The students will:
—describe a way they manage stress.
—discuss the importance of taking responsibility for one's own well-being.

Introduce the Topic:

Say to the students: *Our topic for this circle session is a very useful one because it gives us a chance to talk about things we do that help us get rid of stress and enjoy life. It's also going to allow us to pick up some good tips from each other on how to be our own best friend. The topic is, "Something I Do for My Own Well-Being."*

Most of us find ways to be good to ourselves, but with all the stress each one of us has to deal with, the more ideas we can get for managing stress, the better. Think about things you do for yourself to be healthy, to relax, play, or feel good in general. Perhaps you have a special time when you go off alone to think calmly and take in pleasant surroundings. Maybe you have a form of exercise you do that helps you get rid of tension and allows you to rest very well afterward. You may enjoy losing yourself in some kind of creative activity that relieves built-up stress. Whatever it is, we'd enjoy hearing about it. The topic is, "Something I Do for My Own Well-Being."

Discussion Questions:

1. *Who has the most influence on how well or how poorly you manage your stress levels?*
2. *What similarities did you notice in the methods that were mentioned?*
3. *What new ideas did you get for managing stress?*
4.

One of My Regular Health Habits

Objectives:

The students will:
—examine healthful habits they have acquired.
—state that they are responsible for their own health.

Introduce the Topic:

Our circle session topic for today is, "One of My Regular Health Habits." Each one of us does a lot of things for our health. Maybe you do yoga or exercises each morning when you get out of bed, bicycle or run on the track daily, eat low fat foods, or take vitamins. Perhaps you do things for your mental or emotional health, like reading books that inspire you, meditating, or attending spiritual gatherings regularly. Or maybe you brush and floss your teeth regularly and always keep your body clean.

You may also be doing something so routine that you don't think of it in the context of maintaining health. For example, maybe you walk through a canyon or park on your way to school and, besides regular exercise, you get a spiritual lift from the beauty around you. Maybe you regularly get together with friends to watch a TV sitcom, see a funny movie, or tell jokes. Take a minute to think about your own habits, and choose one to describe for us. The topic is, "One of My Regular Health Habits."

Discussion Questions:

1. Why is it important to take responsibility for your own health at a young age?
2. What habits do you need to change in order to be more healthy?
3. If you want advice about wellness or fitness, with whom do you talk?

I Wanted To Be Part of a Group, But Was Left Out

Objectives:

The students will:
—describe a personal experience in which they were excluded or rejected.
—verbalize negative feelings associated with being left out.
—discuss ways of dealing with rejection.

Introduce the Topic:

Say to the students: *Today's topic is, "I Wanted to Be Part of a Group, But Was Left Out." Think of a time when you had your hopes set on being with a certain group of people—a club, an organization, or a bunch of friends—but it didn't happen. What were the dynamics of the situation? What happened to cause your exclusion? Perhaps it was an event that had been planned very carefully, or maybe it was just a spur-of-the-moment activity. Did something unexpected come up, or did you kind of know you might be left out? Take a moment and trace in your mind the sequence of events leading up to your being excluded. What feelings did you have when you thought you were going to be with this group? What were your feelings later? The topic for today is, "I Wanted to Be Part of a Group, But Was Left Out."*

Note: Since this is a challenging topic, consider taking your turn first.

Discussion Questions:

1. *When you found out you weren't going to be included, how did you feel?*
2. *What did you feel like doing, and what did you actually do?*
3. *Was one of the common reactions to not being included a desire to find someone to blame? Does this help?*
4. *What would help?*

A Time I Felt Like I Belonged

Objective:

The students will describe the importance of belonging and feeling accepted.

Introduce the Topic:

Say to the students: *Our topic today is, "A Time I Felt Like I Belonged." When we talk about belonging to something, it doesn't always have to be an organized group or club; it can just be a group of friends that gets together to do things we like to do. So think of a time you were accepted or included in a group or an activity that was really good for you. How did it happen, and what did it feel like after you were an accepted member? Did someone do something special to give you a comfortable feeling? What gave you a sense of belonging? Maybe you had a secure feeling just because you were with friends, or maybe something else about the time and place gave you that feeling. The topic for today is, "A Time I Felt Like I Belonged."*

Discussion Questions:

1. Was this group or activity something for which you had to try out or have certain qualities or abilities?
2. Why is membership in a group important to most people?
3. When is being in a group undesirable?

One of the Best Times I Ever Had with a Friend

Objectives:

The students will:
—describe qualities of effective peer relationships.
—identify positive feelings engendered by friendship.

**Introduce
the Topic:**

Say to the students: *Our topic today is, "One of the Best Times I Ever Had with a Friend." Most people find that having friends means sharing fun and other kinds of experiences with a person we like. Can you think of a time when you and a friend did something together that was particularly enjoyable? Perhaps you went on a trip together, or played a game, or just relaxed and talked for awhile. What did you do, and how did you feel doing it together? Take a moment or two to think about it. The topic is, "One of the Best Times I Ever Had with a Friend."*

**Discussion
Questions:**

1. *What was more important—the activity you did or the fact that you did it with a friend?*
2. *How do you feel when you're with a friend?*
3. *Why is it that, with friends, good times can be simple— they don't have to involve exciting places and spending lots of money?*

What I Like Best About the Person I Like Most

Objective:

The students will identify desirable qualities and behaviors of friends.

Introduce the Topic:

Say to the students: *Today our topic is, "What I Like Best About the Person I Like Most." This calls for a description of the behavior of someone very special to you, and you may need to give the matter some thought. What are the things this friend of yours does that you really like? In your relationship with this person, what are the best things that have happened between the two of you? Maybe your friend is always ready to do whatever you want to do, or maybe the generous side of your friend is what stands out. Perhaps you can always count on this person to be honest with you or stick up for you. Or maybe your friend makes life more pleasant for you in little ways. See if you can pick out one way this person pleases you very much. The topic is, "What I Like Best About the Person I Like Most."*

Discussion Questions:

1. Can you give us an example of a time when your friend stood up for you or helped you in some way?

2. Are people born with the qualities and behaviors that we discussed? If not, how can we learn them?

3. Do really good friends always do things our way? ...always insist on having their way? Explain.

4. How do you and your best friend handle disagreements?

How I Handled a Disagreement with a Friend

Objectives:

The students will:
—describe conflict situations involving peers.
—explain strategies for resolving conflicts with peers.

Introduce the Topic:

Say to the students: *All of us at one time or another have probably disagreed with a friend and had negative feelings as a result. So today let's talk about those times. Our topic is, "How I Handled a Disagreement with a Friend."*

The disagreement you describe may have been a major thing that led to the end of the friendship, or it may have been resolved in such a way that your friendship became even stronger. You can describe a disagreement that happened to you and a friend when you were children, or one that occurred very recently. The disagreement may have built up over a long period, or it may have been a one-of-a-kind situation that cropped up very suddenly. Try to recreate in your mind what happened, and <u>without telling us the name of your friend</u>, describe the situation and what you did. The topic is, "How I Handled a Disagreement with a Friend."

Discussion Questions:

1. *What are the most common feelings that disagreements generate?*
2. *What were some of the main differences you noticed in the situations described?*
3. *How do you usually respond to disagreements?*
4. *What strategies did you learn from this session that will help you handle future disagreements?*

Someone I Know Who Is an Accepting Person

Objectives:

The students will:
—describe the positive qualities of people they know whose behavior is nonjudgmental and nonevaluative.
—explore the positive feelings that accepting people inspire in them.

Introduce the Topic:

Our topic for today is, "Someone I Know Who Is an Accepting Person." One of the interesting things about knowing an accepting person is that you usually feel good when you're around him or her. Do you know why? An accepting person lets you be you and accepts all the things you are — your strengths and your weaknesses. He or she doesn't judge you, doesn't stereotype you, and doesn't label you.

Think of such a person in your life — someone who accepts you just the way you are. This person might be a parent, friend, teacher, brother or sister, doctor — anyone you know. What does this person do or say that causes you to feel accepted? How do you feel about this person? Take a minute to think about it. The topic is, "Someone I Know Who Is an Accepting Person."

Discussion Questions:

1. *What are some ways that people show acceptance?*
2. *How do you act when you are around a person who is nonjudgmental?*
3. *What is the opposite of accepting? How do you act when you are around someone who is unaccepting?*

Someone Who Trusts Me

Objectives:

The students will:

—describe the positive feelings they experience when they earn someone's trust and validation.

—define trust and explain how it develops between people.

Introduce the Topic:

Today, we are going to discuss trust in our circle session. Our topic is, "Someone Who Trusts Me." Think of a person who trusts you, and tell us how your earned that trust. The person could be a parent, friend, relative, teacher, or employer.

Did this person always trust you, or did you have to prove that you were trustworthy? Maybe you showed that you could be trusted to take care of a younger brother or sister. Perhaps you showed your boss that you could be trusted to always show up on time and work hard until you leave. Or you might have earned the trust of a friend or parent by always telling the truth, even when it might get you in trouble. How do you feel knowing that you are trusted by this person? How does it affect your relationships with other people? Take a minute to think about it, and then let's talk about, "Someone Who Trusts Me."

Discussion Questions:

1. What is trust?

2. How do you learn to trust another person?

3. Is trust always mutual? Why or why not?

4. What kinds of things can destroy trust?

When Someone Expected the Very Best of Me

Objectives:

The students will:

—describe an incident in which someone had high expectations of them.

—explore ways in which the expectations of others influence their behavior.

Introduce the Topic:

Our session for today is all about expectations. The topic is, "When Someone Expected the Very Best of Me." Can you think of a time when you were expected to do your very best at something? This incident may have occurred a long time ago or very recently, and it may involve any kind of situation. You might have been expected to perform well in an athletic event, a game, some kind of project or assignment you were involved in at school, or something you were doing with your friends. The important thing to consider is how you were affected by the person who expected you to do your best. Did you feel good about this person's faith in you, or was the pressure uncomfortable? Maybe you felt both ways at the same time. Take a minute to think it over and, if you will, tell us what happened and how you felt. The topic for today's session is, "When Someone Expected the Very Best of Me."

Discussion Questions:

1. How did most of us perform when someone expected us to do well?

2. When someone expects a person to do poorly, what generally happens? Why?

3. What have you learned about how people influence each other from this session?

Someone Did Something for Me That I Really Appreciated

Objectives:

The students will:
—explore positive feelings they experienced as a result of someone's kindness.
—describe how thoughtful deeds benefit both giver and receiver.

Introduce the Topic:

The topic of this session is, "Someone Did Something for Me That I Really Appreciated." You've probably all been on the receiving end of many thoughtful gestures. Think back over some of those experiences and choose one to share with us. Maybe a friend offered to give you a ride when you needed one, or helped you finish a report that you were struggling with. Perhaps a visiting relative presented you with a special treat, like your favorite cookie, candy, or snack. Or maybe someone listened when you needed to talk about a problem. Think for a moment about something like this that has happened to you. If you told the person how you felt, share that with us, too. The topic for today is, "Someone Did Something for Me That I Really Appreciated."

Discussion Questions:

1. Did you notice any similarities in the kinds of things we appreciated?
2. How are people able to influence each other's feelings?
3. Wisdom says that one way to cheer yourself up when you're feeling low is to do something for someone else. What do you think of that idea?

When Someone Criticized Me

Objectives:

The students will:
—describe a situation in which they were criticized.
—examine the various ways criticism can affect people.
—distinguish between helpful and hurtful criticism.

**Introduce
the Topic:**

In this session, we're going to focus on the effects of criticism. The topic is, "When Someone Criticized Me." Remember a time when someone criticized you and try to recall how you felt when it happened. Also, think about the situation and what was going on that brought about the criticism. Did you get a poor report card, fail to keep a promise, or say something thoughtless? Or did the criticism have to do with your clothes, hairstyle, or some other aspect of your appearance?

How did you feel about the criticism? Perhaps you felt it was unjustified or too harsh — not helpful at all. Or maybe you gained somehow because of the criticism. Were the intentions of the person offering the criticism positive, or was this person being picky or cruel? Take a minute to think about it, and if you will, tell us about a time like this in your life. The topic is, "When Someone Criticized Me."

**Discussion
Questions:**

1. *What methods of offering suggestions or criticism tend to be most effective? ...least effective?*
2. *What is meant by the term constructive criticism?*
3. *If you have trouble receiving criticism, how can you learn to handle it better?*

Something I Never Do When I Want to Make Friends with Someone

Objectives:

The students will:

—identify behaviors that are not conducive to establishing friendships.

—make connections between their behaviors and the degree of success they experience in relationships.

Introduce the Topic:

Today our topic is, "Something I Never Do When I Want to Make Friends with Someone." What things do you purposely avoid doing if you like someone? Being aware of what turns people off and what makes them like you is difficult sometimes, because people are all so different. But most of us have a pretty good idea what we don't like, so that's a good place to start. Maybe you try very hard not to make a pest of yourself when you're getting to know someone. Perhaps you avoid asking too many probing questions, giving advice, talking too much about yourself, or gossiping about the person when he or she isn't around. Think about it for a moment. The topic is, "Something I Never Do When I Want to Make Friends with Someone."

Discussion Questions:

1. *What similarities did you notice in the behaviors we try to avoid.*
2. *How can you recognize the effects of your behavior on others?*
3. *What are some good things to do when a new friendship is first forming.*

One of the Nicest Things a Friend Ever Did for Me

Objectives:

The students will:
—verbalize their feelings concerning a friend's welcome deed or gesture.
—explore some of the qualities of positive friendships.

Introduce the Topic:

Today, we're going to talk about friendships and what they mean to us. The topic is, "One of the Nicest Things a Friend Ever Did for Me." Think back over all of the things your friends have done for you and pick one that gives you particular warmth and pleasure. It might have been planned ahead of time, like a birthday party or special outing, or maybe it was spontaneous, like a sudden compliment or pledge of enduring friendship. Has a friend ever loaned you a favorite article of clothing, compact disk, or cassette; sat with you for hours while you waited for some important news; or offered to help you get your chores done so you could both go to movie? Tell us what your friend did and how you felt about it. The topic is, "One of the Nicest Things a Friend Ever Did for Me."

Discussion Questions:

1. How did your friend seem to feel about the thing he or she did?
2. How did you express your appreciation to your friend?
3. Why are friendships so important in our lives?

Something Nice That I Did for a Friend

Objectives:

The students will:
—acknowledge themselves for one of their own positive behaviors toward a friend.
—identify behaviors that build enduring friendships.

Introduce the Topic:

Sometimes friends do things for us that make us feel good. Today, we're going to give ourselves a pat on the back by talking about our own good deeds. The topic is, "Something Nice That I Did for a Friend."

Maybe you helped your friend do some research for a term paper; loaned him or her a book or article of clothing; took care of your friend's pet while he or she was away on vacation; or invited some friends over and fixed your friend a special birthday breakfast or lunch. Keep in mind that many of the greatest acts of generosity don't involve money at all. They involve our time, attention, and understanding. Think about it for a moment, and tell us about a time when you demonstrated what a good friend you are. The topic is, "Something Nice That I Did for a Friend."

Discussion Questions:

1. *How did your friend feel about what you did? What did he or she do?*
2. *Why is it important for friends to do little things for each other once in awhile?*
3. *What have you learned about friendship from this session?*

I Have a Friend Who Is Really Different From Me

Objectives:

The students will:
—identify areas of difference between themselves and their friends.
—describe ways in which differences contribute to productive, rewarding relationships.

Introduce the Topic:

Our topic for this circle session is, "I Have a Friend Who Is Really Different From Me." Being yourself is an important theme that crops up in life over and over again. Compromising yourself means selling out your real self to some extent just to please someone else. Being yourself means that you will always be different from other people in certain ways. And it also means that they will be different from you when they are being themselves.

Think of a friend who is really different from you. The differences may be external — like skin color, size, or physical appearance — or internal, like viewpoints, values, abilities, or ways of reacting. Does a friend come to mind? Think about it for a few moments. The topic is, "I Have a Friend Who Is Really Different From Me."

Discussion Questions:

1. *What makes a friendship work between two people who are really different?*
2. *Why do we sometimes hide parts of our real selves when we are with our friends?*
3. *How can you let someone know that you appreciate the unique things about him or her?*

How I Learned to Get Along with Someone Who Doesn't Think the Way I Do

Objectives:

The students will:

—describe how they get along with a person whose values and beliefs are different from their own.

—discuss the benefits of being able to get along with people of diverse values/beliefs.

Introduce the Topic:

The topic of this session is, "How I Learned to Get Along with Someone Who Doesn't Think the Way I Do." We've all had experiences where we've had to get along with people who don't think the way we do. Quite often these situations involve our employers and co-workers. Similar situations may occur in our own families.

Think of one person you learned to get along with who didn't think the way you did. How did you overcome this barrier? Did you hide your own feelings and thoughts? Did you try to get your way by using tricks or games? Or did you accept the person and feel acceptance from him or her? If you decide to share, tell us what you did and why you think your approach worked, without telling us the name of the person. Our topic is, "How I Learned to Get Along with Someone Who Doesn't Think the Way I Do."

Discussion Questions:

1. What did you hear in this session that might be useful to you in learning to get along with others?

2. What would life be like if all people were the same?

3. How do we benefit from accepting and even encouraging diverse points of view?

A Time I Was Rejected for Something About Me That Was Different

Objectives:

The students will:

—describe situations in which they were rejected because of something that is part of them.

—identify some of the feelings that rejection evokes.

—discuss prejudice and explain how it relates to incidents of rejection.

Introduce the Topic:

Our topic today is, "A Time I Was Rejected for Something About Me That Was Different." All of us have experienced rejection from time to time. The kind of rejection we're going to discuss today occurs as a reaction to differences between one person and another. Has this ever happened to you? The "something different" for which you were rejected might have been your religion, your viewpoints on a subject, your racial or cultural background, your disability, your age, sex, appearance, or clothing. It might even have been the way you talk, walk, or dance. If you decide to share in this session, tell us about what happened, but please don't mention names. The topic is, "A Time I Was Rejected for Something About Me That Was Different."

Discussion Questions:

1. How do you feel when you're rejected by someone?

2. What does prejudice have to do with the things we've shared today?

3. How do you handle rejection? How do you get over it?

4. How can an experience of rejection lead to positive results?

I Didn't Get Help When I Needed It Badly

Objectives:

The students will:
—describe the feelings of frustration, anger, and helplessness that result from being denied needed help.
—identify the kinds of situations in which help is needed.
—explore circumstances under which they might be of help to others.

Introduce the Topic:

Our topic today is, "I Didn't Get Help When I Needed It Badly." Can you think of a time when you were stuck, or stranded, or hurting, and couldn't get anyone to help you? Maybe your bike or car broke down miles from home and no one would stop to help you. Or maybe you had tried every solution you could think of to a math problem, but couldn't get the teacher to respond to your requests for assistance. Perhaps you were physically sick or injured, or emotionally troubled, but no one seemed to take you very seriously. Have you ever been desperate for a loan, an article of clothing, a visit to a doctor, or a shoulder to cry on? How do you feel and what to you do when you can't get the help you need. When you share, please don't mention any names. The topic is, "I Didn't Get Help When I Needed It Badly."

Discussion Questions:

1. Why do you think the help you needed was denied?
2. How could you have been more assertive in asking for help?
3. What have you learned during this session that might make you a more effective helper?

I Observed a Conflict

Objectives:

The students will:
—describe a conflict situation they observed.
—discuss the dynamics of conflict.
—describe feelings generated in conflict situations.

**Introduce
the Topic:**

Say to the students: *Today we're going to talk about conflict situations we've witnessed. Our topic is, "I Observed a Conflict." There probably isn't anyone here who hasn't at some point in his or her life watched some kind of conflict taking place. A conflict can have many forms. It can be a clash of ideas or needs, either inside a person or involving at least one other person. Or it can be a fight or an argument involving some kind of physical or verbal violence or the threat of it. Without actually telling us who was involved in the conflict you saw, or your relationship to them, tell us what happened, if you will. The topic is, "I Observed a Conflict."*

**Discussion
Questions:**

1. *What are some of the main reasons we have conflicts?*
2. *What patterns do conflict situations seem to take?*
3. *Why is it sometimes difficult to think rationally when you get involved in an upsetting conflict situation?*
4. *Do you think anybody ever wins the kinds of conflicts we have been discussing? Why or why not?*

I Got Blamed for Something I Didn't Do

Objectives:

The students will:
—describe a situation in which they were wrongly accused.
—describe effective ways of responding to false accusations.

Introduce the Topic:

Say to the students: *Our circle session topic today is a challenging one. It's about one of the most distressing things that can happen to a person. The topic is, "I Got Blamed for Something I Didn't Do." Probably everyone has had this happen at least once and it can certainly be upsetting.*

So give it some thought. Maybe you denied having done the thing you were being blamed for, and your denial was accepted. Or perhaps you denied it, and the other people involved didn't believe you. Whatever happened, if you'd like to tell us about it, we'd appreciate hearing. Tell us what happened, and how you felt, but don't mention any names. Our topic is, "I Got Blamed for Something I Didn't Do."

Discussion Questions:

1. *Why is it so upsetting to be blamed for something you didn't do?*
2. *How can you handle a situation in which you are wrongly blamed?*
3. *What does this session teach us about blaming?*

A Time Someone Put Me Down, But I Handled It Well

Objective:

The students will describe how they handled a potential conflict situation positively.

Introduce the Topic:

Begin the session by saying: *Our topic for today is, "A Time Someone Put Me Down, But I Handled It Well." Think about a situation in which you were criticized, ridiculed, ignored, or in some other way diminished, but you managed to maintain your dignity and didn't let it upset you too much. You may have been an adult at the time, or a child. Perhaps you broke something, or made a mistake, or behaved awkwardly, and even though your behavior was unintentional, someone put you down for it. What did the other person say or do? Were there other people present? How did you feel, and what you do to control your reactions? Without mentioning any names, tell us about, "A Time Someone Put Me Down, But I Handled It Well."*

Discussion Questions:

1. *How do you feel about that person now?*
2. *Why do we sometimes enjoy putting each other down?*
3. *When seemingly harmless put downs turn into serious conflicts, what can we do?*
4. *Why are put downs frequently veiled with humor? For whom are they funny?*

A Time I Was Involved in a Misunderstanding

Objectives:

The students will:
—describe how a misunderstanding can lead to conflict.
—discuss ways of effectively handling misunderstandings.

Introduce the Topic:

Begin the session by saying: *Today the topic is, "A Time I Was Involved in a Misunderstanding." Think of a time when you got into a conflict with someone, based on a misunderstanding. Maybe you said something that was understood as a put down when you intended it as a joke. Perhaps you didn't call someone, or were accused of talking behind a friend's back, or said something to one person that was misquoted to another. Maybe you made a gesture or a face that was misunderstood and caused someone to react in anger. Or perhaps someone else did something like this and you were the one who misunderstood. Think about it for a few moments. Then tell us about an incident like that in your life, and how you handled it. The topic is, "A Time I Was Involved in a Misunderstanding."*

Discussion Questions:

1. *When you realize that you have misunderstood someone, what can you do to help clear up the problem?*
2. *What can you do when it appears that someone has misunderstood something you have said or done?*
3. *What causes us to misunderstand the words and actions of others?*

Something That Really Bothers Me

Objectives:

The students will:
—describe things that typically annoy and upset them.
—discuss ways of handling irritations and annoyances to avoid conflict.

**Introduce
the Topic:**

Begin the session by saying: *Today our topic is, "Something That Really Bothers Me." Most of us can name one or more things that are guaranteed to annoy or upset us. What's one of yours? Maybe you're bothered by people who smoke—or people who criticize smokers. Perhaps you're bothered by loud television commercials, or dirty dishes in the sink, or the sound of chalk scraping across the chalkboard. Does dishonesty upset you? Are you annoyed by people who don't pay attention in class? Think it over, and tell us what bothers you—and how you handle your feelings. The topic is, "Something That Really Bothers Me."*

**Discussion
Questions:**

1. *Since the thing that bothers you isn't likely to go away, what can you do to control your feelings?*
2. *Have you ever become involved in a conflict because of the thing that bothers you? How did it happen?*
3. *How much stress do you experience from things that "bother" you? What stress management techniques do you use?*

A Time When Someone Wouldn't Listen to Me

Objectives:

The students will:
—describe how poor communication contributes to conflict.
—discuss the importance of listening, to effective human relations.

Introduce the Topic:

Begin the session by saying: *Today our topic is, "A Time When Someone Wouldn't Listen to Me." Did you ever want very much for someone to listen to you, but they wouldn't do it? Maybe you tried to explain to your parents why you got a certain grade, or arrived home late, or didn't get your chores done—and they wouldn't listen. Or perhaps you wanted to talk to a friend about something that was troubling you, but he or she was too busy to listen. Sometimes when we find ourselves in conflict situations and try to explain our side of it, the other person refuses to listen. Think of a time something like this happened to you. How did you feel, and what did you do? Please don't mention any names. The topic is, "A Time When Someone Wouldn't Listen to Me."*

Discussion Questions:

1. *What feelings do you get when you want someone to listen to you and he or she won't?*
2. *What can you do to get someone to listen to you?*
3. *How does this topic make you feel about listening to others?*

A Time I Controlled Myself and the Situation Well

Objectives:

The students will:
—describe a conflict situation in which they acted responsibly.
—discuss the importance of self-control in conflict situations.

Introduce the Topic:

Say to the students: *Today we have another challenging circle session topic. It is, "A Time I Controlled Myself and the Situation Well." This session gives you a chance to take some deserved credit for handling a difficult circumstance with a cool head. Can you think of a time when you did that?*

Give it some thought. Perhaps you can remember a time when two or more people were upset with each other, or with you, but you were able to remain calm enough to keep the situation from getting out of hand. Perhaps you were afraid that someone might get hurt, so you found some inner confidence and handled things in a way that you're proud of now. Tell us what happened and how you felt, but please don't mention any names. The topic is, "A Time I Controlled Myself and the Situation Well."

Discussion Questions:

1. *How do you feel now about what you did in that situation?*
2. *How do you feel when you lose control of yourself or a situation?*
3. *How can you handle a situation well if you are not in control of yourself?*
4. *What good ideas did you get for handling difficult situations from this session?*

Something I Enjoy Doing Because It Gives Me a Feeling of Accomplishment

Objective:

The students will describe personal accomplishments and the feelings they generate.

Introduce the Topic:

Say to the students: *Today we're going to discuss things we're good at. The topic is, "Something I Enjoy Doing Because It Gives Me a Feeling of Accomplishment." Notice that you're asked to brag a little here, and that's OK. You aren't boasting, and you're not comparing yourself to others or putting anyone else down. You're just telling about what you can do that you're proud of. So think about one thing you like to do that gives you a good feeling. This can be something you enjoy doing at school or away from school. It can be something you've only done once, or an activity you engage in frequently. Think about it for a minute. The topic is, "Something I Enjoy Doing Because It Gives Me A Feeling of Accomplishment."*

Discussion Questions:

1. *What is it about the activity you shared that gives you such good feelings?*
2. *How important is it to experience feelings of accomplishment?*
3. *Did you learn anything new and interesting about anyone in this session?*
4. *What did you learn about yourself?*

Something I'd Do If I Knew I Couldn't Fail

Objectives:

The students will
—identify goals.
—describe how fear can get in the way of reaching a goal.

**Introduce
the Topic:**

Say to the students: *Our topic for this session is, "Something I'd Do If I Knew I Couldn't Fail." Think of something you would do if you knew you absolutely couldn't fail. Perhaps you'd try out for a team, become a circus clown, put an end to world hunger, make a special friend, or become an honor student. You could do this thing strictly for yourself, or you could choose something that would benefit others too. Take some quiet moments and let your imagination play with the idea of guaranteed success. The topic is, "Something I'd Do If I Knew I Couldn't Fail."*

**Discussion
Questions:**

1. What kinds of things did most of us want to do?
2. What's stopping you from doing the thing you described?
3. How can you turn your dreams into goals that you will work toward?
4. What steps can we take to overcome our fears of failure?

Something I Did (or Made) That I'm Proud Of

Objectives:

The students will:
—identify personal accomplishments.
—describe the feelings generated by accomplishments.

Introduce the Topic:

Say to the students: *Our topic for today is, "Something I Did (or Made) That I'm Proud Of." We've all done something, or made something, of which we've been proud. Think of an example in your life, and tell us about it. Maybe the thing that comes to mind makes you proud because other people thought well of you for achieving it. Or perhaps your accomplishment is something no one knows about except you. Perhaps you helped someone who really needed and wanted help, and giving that help made you feel proud of yourself. Or maybe you made something like a perfect fried egg, or fixed something, like a machine, and doing that made you feel proud of yourself. Think for a minute and see if you can come up with something. It can be an accomplishment from your childhood or something you've done recently. The topic is, "Something I Did (or Made) That I'm Proud Of."*

Discussion Questions:

1. Who besides yourself was proud of you? How did he or she show it?

2. How important is it for people to feel proud of themselves?

3. Have you ever felt it wasn't good to feel proud of yourself? If so, what caused you to feel that way?

4. How does pride in ourselves help us continue to accomplish things?

Something I Created

Objective:

The students will describe specific inventions or creative endeavors.

Introduce the Topic:

Our topic for this session is, "Something I Created." Can you think of a time when you created or invented something completely new or uniquely your own? It might have been a piece of artwork, or a Halloween costume, or the decorations on a cake. Perhaps you invented a new trick to do on your bike or skateboard. Or maybe you thought of a new strategy for winning a video game. Your creation could be anything as small as a cure for hiccoughs to as large as a prize-winning short story. Let's take a few moments to think about it. The topic is, "Something I Created."

Discussion Questions:

1. How do you feel when you create or invent something?
2. Maybe doing something creative is the best way to experience a natural high. What do you think?
3. How could we be more creative, more of the time?

Something I Learned That Was Enjoyable

Objectives:

The students will:
—describe a learning activity that gave them satisfaction.
—explore a variety of learning contexts, and discuss how
  they appeal to different people.

**Introduce
the Topic:**

*Today, we're going to look at how learning takes place
and how people acquire skills and knowledge. Learning is
going on all the time for all of us. In fact, we are here in
school because of society's goal to promote learning. Our
topic is, "Something I Learned That Was Enjoyable."*

*Think about a learning experience that was enjoyable for
you — something that you got a lot of pleasure in learning
about. Maybe you enjoyed learning to skate or play
tennis, or perhaps you enjoyed learning to speak a second
language or solve a particular type of math problem. It
could have been something you learned at school, but not
necessarily. Part of what made it enjoyable may have
been the way you learned, not just what was learned. Or
perhaps the most enjoyable thing was the fascinating
nature of the information or the skill itself. If you would
like to share in this session, take a moment to think
and then tell us about, "Something I Learned That Was
Enjoyable."*

**Discussion
Questions:**

*1. What similarities did you notice in the kinds of things we
   enjoyed learning?*
2. What can make a learning situation unenjoyable?
*3. How much of your learning takes place at school?
   ...away from school?*

A Skill I'm Learning Now That I Didn't Have a Year Ago

Objectives:

The students will:
—identify a skills/knowledge they are currently acquiring.
—describe how they contribute to their own intellectual growth.

Introduce the Topic:

During today's session, we're going to talk about things that we are in the process of learning. Our topic is, "A Skill I'm Learning Now That I Didn't Have a Year Ago." Sometimes we don't realize how successful we are in growing until we look at the changes. Is there something you've been learning how to do recently that you weren't even trying a year ago? This could be something that shows on the outside, like learning how to drive, use a computer, or make something with your hands. Or it could be something that doesn't show, like learning how to control yourself, be more sensitive to the feelings of others, or finish your school assignments on time. Take a moment to think about it. Decide on one skill or ability you've developed, and tell us what it is. The topic for today's session is, "A Skill I'm Learning Now That I Didn't Have a Year Ago."

Discussion Questions:

1. *Who decided that you should learn the skill you're currently working on, you or someone else? How does that affect your ability to learn?*
2. *Why do feelings of frustration frequently precede accomplishments?*
3. *Does it matter that certain abilities are more noticeable than others? Why or why not?*

Something I Finished That I Had a Hard Time Starting

Objective:

The students will describe thoughts and attitudes that facilitate goal attainment.

Introduce the Topic:

Say to the students: *Our circle session topic for today is, "Something I Finished That I Had a Hard Time Starting." Do you remember the story of "The Little Engine That Could?" You probably heard it as a child. It was about the little red engine that managed to chug its way over a high mountain because it was sure it could do it. We've all experienced times when we took on something that seemed much too big for us, or when someone else gave us a pretty rough assignment or job. It looked impossible at first, and so it was hard to get started.*

Think of a time like that in your life. Maybe you were given a homework assignment that seemed insurmountable. Or perhaps you were involved in a special project or event that was very involved and complex. Yet, regardless of how difficult it seemed at first, you finished it. Let's take a few moments to think it over. The topic is, "Something I Finished That I Had a Hard Time Starting."

Discussion Questions:

1. *How did your feelings change from the time you began the task till the time you completed it?*
2. *What kinds of attitudes can help a person begin a difficult task?*
3. *Sometimes tasks are easy to start but hard to finish. What attitudes help out in these situations?*

A Project I've Got Going Right Now

Objectives:

The students will:
—describe an ongoing project.
—discuss the importance of working toward goals.

Introduce the Topic:

In your own words, say to the students: *Our topic for this circle session is, "A Project I've Got Going Right Now." You can address this topic in a lot of different ways. For example, your project could be something you are creating. Perhaps you're putting together a bicycle, a quilt, an engine, an article of clothing, an artistic creation, or a musical piece. It could be a problem that you're in the middle of solving, like how you're going to pay for something that you want to buy, or how you can handle a part-time job. It could be a program of self-improvement, too, like going on a diet, or building up your muscles, or improving a specific athletic skill. Looking at life this way, you'll find that you almost always have a project of some kind in progress. What is one of yours ? Think about it for a few moments. Our topic is, "A Project I've Got Going Right Now."*

Discussion Questions:

1. How do you generally feel when you're involved in your project?
2. Why do you think personal projects are so important to people?
3. How do you think being involved in projects now helps you prepare for the future?

Something I Taught Myself

Objectives:

The students will:
—describe a skill or ability they acquired through their own efforts.
—explore the role of self-motivation in the learning process.

Introduce the Topic:

Our topic for today's circle is "Something I Taught Myself." The concept of self-teaching is very important, because when we make the personal effort, we can learn many things on our own. In fact, we learn very few things without deciding to, so in a sense self-teaching is involved in all learning. Think of a skill or ability that you acquired pretty much on your own. Maybe you learned how to use a computer software program or play a video game on your own. Perhaps you taught yourself how to type, draw, ski, cook, or play the piano. Or as a small child, maybe you taught yourself how to read by sounding out the words in storybooks before you ever started school. Think about it for a few moments. Tell what you learned and how you felt about your accomplishment. The topic is, "Something I Taught Myself."

Discussion Questions:

1. How did most of us seem to feel about learning something on our own?
2. How does learning something on your own affect your ability to remember it?
3. How can you learn to summon the same kind of motivation for tasks that you have to learn?

A Time I Taught Something to Someone Else

Objectives:

The students will:
—identify occasions when they have acted as teachers.
—describe some of the ways in which knowledge is shared.

Introduce the Topic:

Today, we're going to talk about something that you learned so well you were able to teach it. The topic is, "A Time I Taught Something to Someone Else."

There are many situations in which people learn. Learning and teaching happen all the time. Think about one time when you were the teacher and you showed someone a skill, or provided a person with some information. This person could have been younger than you, like a child to whom you taught a game. Or it might have been someone your own age, or maybe an older person. Have you ever explained to a classmate how to solve a particular kind of math problem, or how to prepare for a test? Have you ever showed your parent how to use a computer program, or how to do the latest dance step? Think about it for a few moments. The topic is, "A Time I Taught Something to Someone Else."

Discussion Questions:

1. How did your pupil seem to feel about learning from you?
2. When you are teaching someone, which parts of the process are easiest? Which parts are hard?
3. When do people stop teaching and learning? Why?

Something I'm Learning Now That Is Difficult

Objectives:

The students will:
—examine problems they experience learning.
—state that problems with learning are normal and universally experienced.
—explore causes of and remedies for learning problems.

Introduce the Topic:

Today, we are going to talk about times when learning gets tough — and it does for all of us now and then. Our topic is, "Something I'm Learning Now That Is Difficult." Is there anything you are learning at this time, either here at school or somewhere else, that is hard for you? If so, please tell us what it is and what makes it hard. Maybe you are studying a foreign language, and remembering all of the vocabulary and grammar is tough. Perhaps you are having difficulty with math, writing, or physical education. Or maybe the thing that is difficult for you is learning to be on time, make new friends, or control your temper. Practically everything we do involves learning, so difficult learning can occur in almost any area. Think about it for a moment. The topic is, "Something I'm Learning Now That Is Difficult."

Discussion Questions:

1. *What similarities did you notice in the kinds of difficulties we are having?*
2. *What are some of the causes of learning problems?*
3. *What can you do to help yourself learn more easily in the area you mentioned?*

An Experience That Caused Me to See Things Differently

Objectives:

The students will:
—describe an experience that changed their perceptions.
—describe how their perceptions color their experiences and vice versa.

Introduce the Topic:

Today our topic is, "An Experience That Caused Me to See Things Differently." Have you ever thought about how your perceptions affect your experiences and vice versa? Lots of times we interpret events based on beliefs and viewpoints that we already have. Occasionally, an experience can cause us to shift our point of view and see things in a different way. For example, perhaps someone you didn't like very well unexpectedly did you a favor, and suddenly you saw the person as okay. Or maybe an important world event profoundly affected the lives of a lot of people, and made you view your own life differently. Maybe the experience that changed your perception occurred while you were watching a movie, reading a book, working on a project, or trying to solve a tough problem. If you would like to share with the group, tell us about, "An Experience That Caused Me to See Things Differently."

Discussion Questions:

1. Did you notice any similarities in the kinds of experiences that caused us to see things differently?
2. How are our perceptions and belief systems formed in the first place?
3. Why is it difficult for some people to change their perceptions even in the face of overwhelming evidence that says those perceptions are wrong?

Something I See Differently Than My Parents' Generation Sees It

Objectives:

The students will:
—identify an area of general disagreement between younger and older generations.
—describe how experiences shape perceptions.

Introduce the Topic:

Today our topic is, "Something I See Differently Than My Parents' Generation Sees It." The focus of this session is on perceptions and opinions. People's opinions are influenced by their perceptions and vice versa. So it is very natural for people of different generations to see different things in different ways. You probably see some situations in much the same way as your parents see them. You can probably think of other things that you view very differently. Tell us about one of those. Perhaps you think that your generation and the generation of your parents have different ideas about music, entertainment, money, politics, or dating. Think about it for a few moments. The topic is, "Something I See Differently Than My Parents' Generation Sees It."

Discussion Questions:

1. Just for a minute, imagine that you are a member of your parents' generation and that you grew up under the same circumstances as your parents did. How do you think you would see some of the issues that were brought up in this session?

2. Knowing your parents, how do you think they would react if they were growing up now?

Something I Created as a Child

Objectives:

The students will:
—describe a childhood creation and what it meant to them.
—explain the importance of creativity in their present lives.

**Introducing
the Topic:**

*Our circle session topic for today is, "Something I Created
as a Child." Do you have memories of things you used to
do when you were little? Think back and try to remember
some of the things you created. They might have been
creations of your mind, like fantasies or daydreams, objects
that you created with wood or Legos, plays you created
with other children, or characters you created in stories or
with dress-up clothes.*

*Maybe you used to get large cardboard crates or a table
and, with just old sheets and imagination, magically turn
them into castles and forts. Or maybe you created an
imaginary friend who talked only to you and was invisible
to everyone else. Perhaps you were an artist who created
beautiful drawings and paintings. Take a few moments to
think about it and, if you will, tell us about something you
created when you were little. The topic is, "Something I
Created as a Child."*

**Discussion
Questions:**

1. *What similarities did you notice in the ways we felt
   about our childhood creations?*
2. *Why did we do these creative things?*
3. *In what ways are you creative today? How could you be
   more creative?*
4. *What have you learned about creativity from this
   session?*

How My Environment Affects My Creativity

Objectives:

The students will:
—identify elements in their environment that help and hinder their creative endeavors.
—describe specific ways in which they can modify their environment to make it more conducive to creativity.

Introduce the Topic:

Today, we're going to talk about, "How My Environment Affects My Creativity." What kind of an environment helps you create? Maybe you like to work in a quiet place that is beautiful, or perhaps hearing a certain kind of music helps you create. Maybe you prefer to be in the middle of a busy place with a lot of activity going on around you. Or maybe certain people inspire and encourage you, so you like having them around. You can also tell us about things that get in the way of your creativity. Perhaps interruptions that disrupt your creative flow really bother you, or maybe you feel shut down when you're around someone who insists that you do things a certain way. Think about it for a few moments. If you tell about a person who affects you negatively, please don't say his or her name. The topic is, "How My Environment Affects My Creativity."

Discussion Questions:

1. What similarities did you notice in the things that stimulate our creativity? ...hinder our creativity?
2. Why are people's creativity needs different?
3. If you have an environment problem that constantly interferes with your ability to work effectively and creatively, what can you do about it?

The Craziest Dream I Ever Had

Objectives:

The students will:

—describe a dream that contained unusual or "crazy" elements.

—discuss the importance of dreaming to mental and physical health.

Introduce the Topic:

Our circle topic for this session is, "The Craziest Dream I Ever Had." Dreams can help us to see things differently than we see them when we're awake. Some dreams appear very unreal — even crazy. Others give us clues as to what's going on inside us. Still other dreams provide inspiration for creative activities, like writing, painting, or inventing. Maybe you can remember dreams full of color and unusual characters. Perhaps you've had a dream in which you were involved in a long and complicated adventure. Or maybe you've had one of the most common dreams of all — a dream about flying. It's interesting to know that other people have crazy dreams, too. You are invited to share yours with us today. The topic is, "The Craziest Dream I Ever Had."

Discussion Questions:

1. What kinds of insights have you gained or problems have you solved through a dream?

2. Everyone dreams several times every night. Why do you think that is?

3. People whose sleep (and dreaming) is frequently interrupted for several nights in a row sometimes start to act crazy themselves. What connections might there be between our dreams and our mental health?

In My Dream, My Wish Came True

Objectives:

The students will:
—share wishes that they have dreamed about.
—explain how wish-fulfillment dreams satisfy and
motivate.

**Introduce
the Topic:**

*Our topic today is, "In My Dream My Wish Came True."
Dreams can be fun, as all dreamers know. They give us
opportunities to experience things we'd like to experience
that either can't realistically happen or haven't happened
yet. These kinds of dreams are called wish-fulfillment
dreams. Dreams can also give us ideas for marvelous
possibilities that we would never think of when we're
awake. Maybe you dreamed once that you were driving
your favorite car, or visiting someone who lives far away —
or someone who is no longer living. Perhaps you dreamed
that you were getting ready to go out with a person you
always admired, or that you had lots of money to spend
at your favorite store. Think carefully and see if you can
recall a dream in which your wish came true. Tell us about
it, if you will. The topic is, "In My Dream My Wish Came
True."*

**Discussion
Questions:**

1. Of what use is a wish-fulfillment dream?
*2. Have you ever made a wish come true after dreaming
    about it? How?*
3. What did you learn from this session about dreaming?

I Did Something in My Dream That I Couldn't Do Awake

Objectives:

The students will:
—describe dreams in which they have superhuman powers and abilities.
—discuss possible benefits and purposes of incredible dreams.

Introduce the Topic:

Our topic for today is, " I Did Something in My Dream That I Couldn't Do Awake." Have you ever dreamed of doing something powerful, heroic, or exciting that you couldn't really do in everyday life — something such as save the world, fall off a high cliff and not get hurt, take a trip into space, or become as small as an insect or as tall as a skyscraper? What do you suppose was the purpose of your far-fetched dream? Think about is for a moment or two. The topic is, "I Did Something in My Dream That I Couldn't Do Awake."

Discussion Questions:

1. *Were there any parts of the dreams we shared that we could actually do?*
2. *Most dreams are forgotten very quickly. If you want to remember a dream, how do you go about doing so?*
3. *What did you learn about yourself from the dream you shared?*

A Time I Was Glad I Had Supervision

Objectives:

The students will:
—describe a situation in which they needed guidance and supervision to complete a task.
—discuss the positive aspects of being led or supervised.
—suggest ways of seeking supervision when they need it.

Introduce the Topic:

Out topic today is, "A Time I Was Glad I Had Supervision." Frequently, we like doing things without anyone telling us how or when to do them. We can be our own leaders. But there are other times when it's very helpful to have someone there who has the knowledge, the skills, and perhaps even the authority to give us guidelines and helpful suggestions. Can you remember such a time? Maybe you didn't know how to finish a project, were having trouble mastering a difficult move in sports, or were trying to cope with a tough emotional situation. You needed and wanted someone to give you encouragement, show you the next step, coach you while you practiced, or listen and offer advice. Take a minute to think, and see if you can come up with an example from your own experience. The topic is, "A Time I Was Glad I Had Supervision."

Discussion Questions:

1. What similarities did you notice in the situations we described?

2. What would happen if you tried to accomplish something without help when you clearly didn't have the knowledge or skills?

3. When you know you need help and supervision but there's no one around to provide it, how can you go about getting the help you need?

Something at Which I'm Getting Better

Objectives:

The students will:
—identify a current pursuit wherein they have noticed improvement.
—describe the effects of success on motivation and performance.

Introduce the Topic:

Today, our topic asks us to talk about improvement. It is, "Something at Which I'm Getting Better." Think of a skill or ability that you are acquiring right now — one at which you are gradually improving. Maybe it's something you've been working at for a long time, like playing a musical instrument or speaking a second language. On the other hand, perhaps you've only been involved in this activity for a few days or weeks. Are you learning to drive a car? Are you studying dance or acting, trigonometry or physics? Have you recently started keeping a journal or writing articles for the school paper? What are you doing that is helping you improve, and how do you feel when you notice your improvement? Think about it for a few moments. The topic is, "Something at Which I'm Getting Better."

Discussion Questions:

1. Why do people like to know how well they're doing?

2. When you know you are getting better at something, what effect does it have on your performance? ...your motivation?

3. How can you train yourself to take notice of your own improvement so that you can give yourself credit?

Part of Me Wanted to Do One Thing, and Part of Me Wanted to Do Another

Objectives:

The students will:
—describe an inner conflict involving two or more choices.
—identify different parts of their personalities and talk about how those parts relate.

Introduce the Topic:

The topic of this session is, "Part of Me Wanted to Do One Thing, and Part of Me Wanted to Do Another." We've all been torn between two or more choices. When we can't decide, we're being ambivalent. Here's a typical example: One part of you — let's call it the student part — wants to study and learn a subject well. Another part of you — the social part — wants to go to a party. Both parts are very real, but at times they conflict with each other. How many of you have had a similar experience? Maybe part of you wants to go to college and part of you wants to get a job and earn money. Perhaps part of you wants to join a particular team, club, or organization, and another part of you says, "don't get involved." Take a minute and think about it and, if you will, tell us about your experience with ambivalence. The topic is, "Part of Me Wanted to Do One Thing, and Part of Me Wanted to Do Another."

Discussion Questions:

1. What causes us to have mixed or conflicting feelings about an issue?
2. When you feel ambivalent about something, how do you handle it?
3. What are the advantages and disadvantages of having many different parts, even when they conflict?

A Time I Shared (or Didn't Share) in Making a Decision

Objectives:

The students will:

—describe decision-making situations and how they were resolved.

—identify some of the benefits and difficulties of shared decision-making.

Introduce the Topic:

Say to the students: *Our topic for this session is, "I Time I Shared (or Didn't Share) in Making a Decision." Think of a time when a decision was being made by a person or group, and because the decision was likely to affect you, you were asked for your opinion. Or, think of a time when a decision was being made that would affect you, and you <u>weren't</u> consulted. Perhaps this was a decision that affected you very much. Did you join in the discussion, or was the decision made <u>for you</u> by someone else? Tell us what happened, whichever way it occurred, and how you felt about it. Please don't name the other people involved. The topic is, "I Time I Shared (or Didn't Share) in Making a Decision."*

Discussion Questions:

1. *What can you do the next time you think you're being left out of a decision that affects you?*
2. *When you are in charge of making a decision that involves other people, how will you handle it?*
3. *What are some of the benefits of shared decision-making? What are some of the difficulties?*

I Used Good Judgment

Objectives:

The students will:
—describe a decision they made.
—define *judgment* and its role in decision-making.

Introduce the Topic:

In your own words, say to the students: *Our topic for this session is, "I Used Good Judgment." The point of this session is to discuss times when we used our judgment to make choices that worked out well for us. No one exercises perfect judgment all the time, but you and I have used good judgment on many occasions. Think of an example. Perhaps you used good judgment in the way you spent some money, or handled a problem, or asked for help in making a difficult decision. Maybe you thought over your decision very carefully, or perhaps you just knew what to do. Regardless of how long it took, or the exact process you used, the results verified that your judgment was sound. If you'd like to tell us about a time when you believe you exercised good judgment, we'd like to hear about it. The topic is, "I Used Good Judgment."*

Discussion Questions:

1. *How did you feel before you decided what to do?*
2. *How did you feel after you decided?*
3. *What constitutes good judgment?*
4. *If a decision doesn't work out the way you thought it would, does that mean you used bad judgment? Why or why not?*
5. *How can a good decision for one person be a bad decision for another?*

A Time When I Didn't Want Anyone Telling Me What to Do

Objective:

The students will:

—describe instances in which they received unnecessary or unwanted supervision.

—differentiate between situations that require supervision and those that don't.

Introduce the Topic:

Today we're going to talk about, "A Time When I Didn't Want Anyone Telling Me What to Do." Remember a time when you were working on something, and you were having a little trouble but pretty much had it under control, when someone came along and began telling you what to do. You've undoubtedly experienced times when you knew that, if you stuck with something long enough, you'd get it. And since getting it on your own was important, outside help was not welcome. Think of an example to share with us. Maybe you were trying to master a particular subject or sport, or perhaps you were repairing your bike or learning a new computer program — and you definitely did not want supervision. The topic is, "A Time When I Didn't Want Anyone Telling Me What to Do."

Discussion Questions:

1. Have you ever tried to supervise someone who didn't want any supervision? What happened?

2. What do you need from other people at times like these?

3. What kinds of situations always require supervision?

4. What can you say to a person who tries to give you advise or supervision that you don't need or want?

Something Worth Saving For

Objectives:

The students will:
—name something valuable enough to save their money for.
—describe what they learn by saving, and how they feel when they do it.

Introduce the Topic:

Our topic for this session is, "Something Worth Saving For." When you save money, obviously that means you can't spend it — at least not for awhile. So it helps to know that what you're saving for is really worth giving up some of your spending power. What do you think is valuable enough to save for? A college education? A special trip? A computer or stereo? A car? It doesn't matter if you are actually saving or not. Just think of something important enough to save for and tell us how you would do it. The topic is, "Something Worth Saving For."

Discussion Questions:

1. *What are the advantages of saving money? What are the disadvantages?*
2. *Why is saving money sometimes so difficult?*
3. *What is it like to wait for something you want very much?*

Someone Handled a Problem Differently Than I Would Have

Objectives:

The students will:

—describe how individuals handle problems and manage areas of their lives in different ways.

—identify some of the benefits of keeping an open mind when confronted with differences in others.

Introduce the Topic:

Today we're going to discuss the topic, "Someone Handled a Problem Differently Than I Would Have." Discovering new things about the people we know makes them interesting to us. We learn the different ways they think and how they react to certain situations. Sometimes the things we observe in others help us change and grow. Think of a time when you observed someone handling a problem very differently than you would have handled it. Maybe a friend was trying to fix something, and he or she went about it in a way that really surprised or puzzled you. Or perhaps a person you know had a problem involving strong emotions and controlled or expressed those feelings in a very unusual way — at least to your way of thinking. Think about it for a few moments. The topic is, "Someone Handled a Problem Differently Than I Would Have."

Discussion Questions:

1. Why do people respond to problems differently?

2. The famous Italian film director, Frederico Fellini, once said, "Accept me as I am; only then will we discover each other." What do you think he meant?

3. What happens to us if we close our minds to ideas and ways of behaving that are different from our own?

I Ignored a Problem, But It Didn't Go Away

Objectives:

The students will:
—examine the possible consequences of ignoring a serious problem.
—identify fears and other factors that lead to ignoring problems, and discuss how to overcome those factors.

Introduce the Topic:

Our topic for this circle session is, "I Ignored a Problem, But It Didn't Go Away." Sometimes problems disappear if we leave them alone. For example, disagreements between people are often forgotten within a few hours or days, and not having a date for a big dance is no longer a problem after the event has passed. However, other kinds of problems don't go away. They keep nagging at us until we resolve them, and sometimes they get worse. Can you think of an example like this? Maybe you lost a library book and put off telling the librarian while the fines mounted. Perhaps you had a health problem that kept getting worse because you didn't see a doctor. Or maybe you ignored an important school project because you didn't know how to get started, and not completing it seriously affected your grade. Think about it for a few moments. Tell us why you ignored the problem and what happened as a result. The topic is, "I Ignored a Problem, But It Didn't Go Away."

Discussion Questions:

1. Why do we sometimes ignore problems that really need our attention?

2. How do you feel when a problem is nagging at you, but you're trying to ignore it?

3. How can you make yourself take that first step toward a resolution?

I Solved a Problem Effectively

Objectives:

The students will:
—describe a problem and its solution.
—verbalize the importance of developing problem-solving skills.
—describe positive feelings associated with successful problem-solving.

Introduce the Topic:

Say to the students: *Our topic today is, "I Solved a Problem Effectively." Since this topic focuses on something you did in the past, take a moment to think back. We're not looking for the spicy, intimate details of your personal past. No true confessions, but rather a problem you had, such as a tough school assignment or some other sort of situation like most of us face every day. Think back to how you recognized the problem, how you faced it, and the feelings that went with handling it successfully. Our topic is, "I Solved a Problem Effectively."*

Discussion Questions:

1. *Was it easy or difficult for you to face this particular problem? What about problems in general?*
2. *Why do people sometimes feel ashamed to have a problem?*
3. *Did it seem to you that members of this group faced similar types of problems? Did we handle them in similar ways?*
4. *How do you feel when you solve a problem effectively?*

When People Try to Solve Each Other's Problems

Objectives:

The students will:
—evaluate solutions to problems.
—describe the importance of solving one's own problems.

Introduce the Topic:

Say to the students: *We have been focusing on different aspects of problem-solving. Today our topic is, "When People Try to Solve Each Other's Problems." Think of a time when a person you know became absorbed in someone else's problem. You may have been one of the people involved. Or maybe you were a witness, and saw a friend or relative offer advice or a solution to another person. Try to remember whether or not the person with the problem asked for help, and whether or not the advice was really helpful. Did the solution offer long-range benefits for the person with the problem, or was it just an unwelcome interference? Remember, this doesn't have to have been an intimate, personal thing—just a time when one person tried to solve another person's problem. If you decide to share, tell us what happened and how each person reacted, without naming those involved. The topic today is, "When People Try to Solve Each Other's Problems."*

Discussion Questions:

1. *What was the attitude of the person who tried to solve the other person's problem?*
2. *How did the person with the problem react when the other person tried to solve it for him or her?*
3. *Why is it easy for the person who doesn't have the problem to know what should be done about it?*
4. *Why is it sometimes very hard for a person who has a problem to figure out what to do?*
5. *If you think you have a suggestion for someone with a problem, what can you say or do?*

A Problem I'd Like Suggestions for Solving

Objectives:

The students will identify and describe a problem and formulate solutions to problems presented by others.

Introduce the Topic:

Say to the students: *Sometimes when people offer advice it can be an annoyance, especially if the advice isn't asked for. But there are times when suggestions may be helpful. So today our topic is, "A Problem I'd Like Suggestions for Solving." The word "suggestion" usually means you can either accept or reject the idea. However, if you ask for a suggestion, it usually means you have a fairly open mind and will at least consider it. Today, each of you is going to have an opportunity to share a problem for which you'd be willing to consider some suggestions. When you receive suggestions, you don't need to comment on them. Acknowledge each suggestion with a thank you. If you give someone a suggestion, don't worry if it doesn't turn out to be the perfect answer. The format for today will be a little different. One person will share a problem; then the rest of us will offer alternatives for that person to consider. If your problem involves other people, please don't mention their names. Take a few moments to think it over. The topic is, "A Problem I'd Like Suggestions for Solving."*

Discussion Questions:

1. *What's different about this exercise and having someone give you advice you didn't ask for?*
2. *Does just having someone listen as you talk about a problem seem to help? Why?*
3. *How did you feel about accepting suggestions from others?*
4. *How did you feel about offering suggestions?*

Note: Limit in advance the amount of time allotted to giving solutions for each problem. Explain to the students that this will ensure everyone's having an opportunity to receive help.

A Time I Talked to Someone I Was Afraid to Talk To

Objectives:

The students will:

—describe how they overcame the fear of talking to an other person.

—identify reasons people fear interacting with others.

—discuss methods of overcoming the fear of interaction.

Introduce the Topic:

Today we're going to talk about, "A Time I Talked to Someone I Was Afraid to Talk To." This is probably one of the most common fears among people — teenagers, little kids, and adults alike. At the same time, it's one of those fears that many people think they alone have! Think back. See if you can remember being almost too intimidated by someone to utter a word, yet somehow overcoming your fear and talking with the person. Perhaps the person was very important, or unpredictable, or in a position to hurt you in some way. Maybe you were afraid that the person wouldn't like you, or that you'd say something stupid. Tell us the circumstances and how you controlled your fear. If the incident involved anyone we know, please don't mention his or her name. The topic is, "A Time I Talked to Someone I Was Afraid to Talk To."

Discussion Questions:

1. How did this person act toward you when you talked to him or her?

2. What feelings did you have before and after you actually spoke to the person?

3. What causes us to feel intimidated by some people?

4. What can you say or do to bolster your courage in such situations?

Someone Tried to Make Me Do Something I Didn't Want to Do

Objectives:

The students will:
—describe a time when they were the object of pressure.
—examine the consequences of bowing to pressure.
—identify methods of resisting pressure from peers and adults.

Introduce the Topic:

Today's topic is, "Someone Tried to Make Me Do Something I Didn't Want to Do." Maybe you can think of a time when someone you knew — a friend perhaps, or a group of friends — wanted you to go someplace or do something that you knew was unwise, illegal, or even risky. Maybe someone asked if he or she could copy a report you wrote. Perhaps a friend pressured you to attend a party that your parents said you couldn't go to. Or maybe someone tried to get you to use alcohol or another drug.

The thing to focus on here is how you handled the situation. Did you go along with the person and, if you did, how did you feel about it later? If you decided not to go along, how did you refuse? If you decide to share your experience, tell us what happened and how you felt, but don't tell us who was pressuring you. The topic for today is, "Someone Tried to Make Me Do Something I Didn't Want to Do."

Discussion Questions:

1. *What makes these seem like "no-win" situations?*
2. *Which matters more — doing what you believe is right or not disappointing the other person?*
3. *What kinds of skills do you need to say no effectively?*

I Said Yes When I Wanted to Say No

Objectives:

The students will:
—describe a time when they failed to assert themselves.
—discuss the dynamics of assertive and submissive behaviors.

Introduce the Topic:

Today we are going to talk about being assertive. The topic is, "I Said Yes When I Wanted to Say No."

Have you ever done this? Perhaps you were asked to do something you really didn't want to do, like go to a movie you didn't want to see, or run an errand for someone. But instead of being assertive and honest, you agreed to do it. Things like this happen all the time. We say yes to work, play, food, games, tobacco, drugs, dates, and all kinds of other things that we really have no interest in. Take a moment to think about a time when something like this happened to you. The topic is, "I Said Yes When I Wanted to Say No."

Discussion Questions:

1. *Why do you think people say yes when they really want to say no?*
2. *If you resent having to do something, but you say yes, who's to blame?*
3. *How can we learn to say no more effectively?*

It Was Hard to Say No, But I Did

Objectives:

The students will:
—describe a time when they were assertive against difficult odds.
—discuss the use of assertive skills in various situations.

Introduce the Topic:

Today we're going to talk about a time when we were assertive — when we stood up for our own wants and feelings. Our topic is, "It Was Hard to Say No, But I Did."

Often we go along with what other people want us to do or believe because it seems like the easiest, most acceptable thing to do. There are times, however, when our convictions tell us to follow a different course. Can you think of a time when you stood up for your own beliefs and feelings? Maybe a close friend asked you to do something, and you hated to disappoint him or her, but you found the courage to say no. Perhaps you were tempted to have a second helping of dessert, but summoned the will power to say no. Or maybe someone asked you to tell a secret, and you were really tempted to talk, but at the last second stopped yourself. Think it over for a minute and then, if you will, tell us about a time like this in your life. The topic is, "It Was Hard to Say No, But I Did."

Discussion Questions:

1. How can you say no effectively, without hurting the other person's feelings?
2. In what kinds of situations is it hardest to be assertive?
3. How can learning to be assertive help you throughout your life?

I Stood Up for Something I Strongly Believe In

Objectives:

The students will:
—describe times when they behaved assertively regarding a strongly held value or principle.
—demonstrate an understanding of assertive versus nonassertive behaviors.

Introduce the Topic:

Many times during our lives, we are given the opportunity to speak out for the things we believe in. Taking a stand can be a difficult experience, especially if friends or relatives don't agree with our position. Even when they do agree, it's not necessarily easy to state our beliefs publicly. Today, we're going to talk about the conviction and determination these situations demand. Our topic is, "I Stood Up for Something I Strongly Believe In."

Perhaps you saw a group of people doing something that you felt was wrong. Maybe you observed some kids teasing or harassing another kid, and intervened. Or maybe, during a conversation about a controversial subject, you stated your beliefs even though everyone else in the group held the opposing view. If you decide to share, please don't mention the names of the other people involved. The topic is, "I Stood Up for Something I Strongly Believe In."

Discussion Questions:

1. As you look back on the situation you shared, how do you feel about it right now?
2. Why is it sometimes hard to stand up for your beliefs?
3. What are the risks and benefits of taking a stand?
4. What are some ills in our society that people need to take a stand against?

A Time When I Was the Leader

Objectives:

The students will:
—describe a time when they took a leadership role.
—explore positive and negative aspects of being a leader.
—name qualities and skills that they think are important in a leader.

Introduce the Topic:

Today we're going to talk about, "A Time When I Was the Leader." Most of us have had one or more experiences with leadership or being in a position of authority. Maybe it was for just a short time, or it might have been for several weeks or months. Perhaps you found yourself in an emergency situation in which you had to take charge. Maybe you were the head of a team, or a study group, or even a group of friends. Or perhaps you were in charge of some small children.

After you think of an example, try to remember what you had to deal with as a leader and how you felt. Did you have to solve problems, inspire others, show people what to do? Did you feel nervous, confident, powerful, or elated? Did you share responsibility with some of your followers, or did you carry the entire burden yourself? Think about it for a few moments. Our topic is, "A Time When I Was the Leader."

Discussion Questions:

1. What were the toughest things about being a leader?
2. What were the advantages and the rewards?
3. What qualities and skills do you think a leader should have?

A Situation in Which I Behaved Responsibly

Objectives:

The students will:
—define responsible behavior.
—describe a situation in which they behaved responsibly.
—discuss the benefits of responsible behavior.

**Introduce
the Topic:**

Say to the students: *Today in our circle session, we are going to take some deserved credit. The topic is, "A Situation in Which I Behaved Responsibly." Before we go any further, let's take a couple of minutes to talk about what responsible behavior is and why people think it's so great. Do you have any ideas?*

Listen to the students' comments. Then, in your own words, explain: *The word itself, <u>response</u>-<u>able</u>, says a lot. It means being **able** to <u>respond</u>, to do something you think is right, not just sit there and do nothing. In other words, when you take care of a situation and yourself, you've behaved responsibly. You can feel proud of yourself. It may have been simple, or it may have been hard, but you did it! Think that over. You can probably remember lots of times when you behaved responsibly. See if there isn't one you'd like to tell us about. If there is, we'd like to hear what happened, how you felt, and what you did. The topic is, "A Situation in Which I Behaved Responsibly."*

**Discussion
Questions:**

1. *How do you feel now about the responsible behavior you described?*
2. *What rewards do you get for responsible behavior?*
3. *What are some of the consequences of irresponsible behavior?*
4. *Did you hear any good ideas for ways to behave responsibly that you might not have thought of before?*

A Way I'm Independent

Objectives:

The students will:
—define the term *independence*.
—describe ways in which they are independent.

Introduce the Topic:

Say to the students: *Today our topic is, "A Way I'm Independent." The word "independent" in this context means that in some part of your life, you have qualified to take responsibility and make decisions, without help from anyone else. Maybe you've found that you can handle a job and school at the same time, or maybe you're quite responsible when it comes to taking care of money. Perhaps you budget your time well, and you don't need reminders anymore about when to do this or that. Whatever way it is that you are now independent, try to remember how you achieved it. Did you have to prove yourself to someone else, or did you develop this independence to please yourself? If you decide to share, tell us how you feel about your new area of responsibility. The topic is, "A Way I'm Independent."*

Discussion Questions:

1. How does a person become independent?
2. How can you become independent in other areas?
3. Why is it hard for others to accept our independence sometimes?
4. Do you think there will be times when you'll wish you could go back to being dependent, just for awhile? Why or why not

How I Helped Someone Who Needed and Wanted My Help

Objectives:

The students will:
—describe incidents in which they played a helping role.
—name some of the characteristics of a helper.

Introduce the Topic:

Say to the students: *Our circle session topic today is, "How I Helped Someone Who Needed and Wanted My Help." Can you think of a time when someone you knew obviously needed help? Perhaps the person was doing something the wrong way and you could see that. But pride or stubbornness or self-determination wouldn't allow him/ her to accept any help. You've also probably experienced times when people really wanted help, but didn't appear to need it. Perhaps they were just a little lazy and wanted your assistance to make things easy.*

But can you think of a time when someone both needed <u>and</u> wanted your help, and you were able to give it? Think about it for a few moments, and tell us about a time this happened in your life. Our topic is, "How I Helped Someone Who Needed and Wanted My Help."

Discussion Questions:

1. How do people generally seem to feel when they get help that is both needed and wanted?
2. What does it take to be a good helper?
3. What feelings did you have when you realized that you could really help someone?

If I Could Do Anything, with No Limits

Objectives:

The students will:
—describe what career they would choose if their possibilities were unlimited.
—describe the relationship between career and lifestyle.

Introduce the Topic:

Say to the students: *Our topic for this session is, "If I Could Do Anything, with No Limits." Too often, we place limits on ourselves. Sometimes those limits are realistic, but often they are not. We block ourselves because of perceived rather than real limitations. One way to discover what we really want in our lives, both personally and professionally, is to consider what we would do if we had no limitations at all. What would you want your job to be if you didn't have to worry about money, education, or training? Maybe you would be a ski instructor and live in the mountains so that your family could grow up in a natural environment. Perhaps you would like to raise horses or take care of sick animals, if you didn't have to worry about buying a ranch or paying for veterinary school. If you didn't have to worry about supporting yourself, maybe you would write a novel, or become an inventor, or work full time raising funds for the homeless. Tell us about the lifestyle and profession you would want if anything were possible. Take a few moments to think it over. The topic is, "If I Could Do Anything, with No Limits."*

1. How much does a person's job determine lifestyle?
2. Does lifestyle determine career, or does career determine lifestyle? How?
3. What happens when we place arbitrary limits on ourselves?
4. How can you plan a career that is compatible with your desired lifestyle?

Where I Think Humankind is Headed

Objective:

The students will describe their feelings and concerns about the future of the human race and then discuss global issues facing humanity.

Introduce the Topic:

Say to the students: *The topic for this session is, "Where I Think Humankind is Headed." In most of our circle sessions in this unit we've been discussing good things that one human being—you by yourself or as a member of a group—has done for other human beings. We've described many wonderful instances of helpfulness and kindness. However, we know that there is a lot of cruelty and greed in the world, as well. There is also much violence and injustice. As you look at the world around you, and the way individuals, societies, and systems act toward one another, the way they compete or cooperate with each other, how do you see the trend running? Think back to what you know of history and where humankind has been in the past. This may help you think about the future. Are you optimistic or pessimistic about the future of humankind? Think about it for a minute. Today's topic is, "Where I Think Humankind is Headed."*

Discussion Questions:

1. *What similarities did you notice in our thoughts and feelings?*
2. *If you could describe the way things are going between people of this world as a season of the year, would it be Spring, Summer, Autumn, or Winter? Why?*
3. *If you were to describe where you think humankind is headed as water, what term would you use to describe the water: "calm," "rough," "stormy," "river," "creek," "ocean," "pond," "lake," etc? Why?*
4. *What do you think are the main issues facing our world?*

Something I've Done (or Could Do) to Improve Our World

Objective:

The students will describe ways in which they can contribute to the betterment of the community/world.

Introduce the Topic:

Say to the students: *The topic for this session is, "Something I've Done (or Could Do) to Improve Our World." Can you think of a time when you did something that you felt really helped, even in a small way, to improve the world we live in? Perhaps you improved a condition of some kind on your street or in your community. Maybe you helped change something that you thought was wrong. Or perhaps you did something to help the ecology—like making careful use of resources like water and electricity, or treating animals with care. Whatever it is, we would like to hear about it. If you can't think of something you've already done, perhaps you can think of something you would like to do in the future, either independently or with a group. Our topic is, "Something I've Done (or Could Do) to Improve Our World."*

Discussion Questions:

1. *How are feelings of apathy developed?*
2. *How can we create an atmosphere in this community/ country that will encourage people to take action to improve things?*
3. *How do you feel when you do something that helps improve our world?*

If your heart is in Social-Emotional
Learning, visit us online.

Come see us at
www.InnerchoicePublishing.com

Our web site gives you a look at all our other Social-Emotional
Learning-based books, free activities, articles, research, and
learning and teaching strategies. Every week you'll get a new
Sharing Circle topic and lesson.

INNERCHOICE Publishing
15079 Oak Chase Court
Wellington, FL 33414

CPSIA information can be obtained
at www.ICGtesting.com
Printed in the USA
FSHW02n0625290718
50712FS